icebox cakes

Also by Lauren Chattman

Mom's Big Book of Cookies

The Cereal Lover's Cookbook

Icebox Desserts

Dessert University (with Roland Mesnier)

Icebox Pies

Mom's Big Book of Baking

Instant Gratification

Just Add Water

Cool Kitchen

LAUREN CHATTMAN

Photography by Duane Winfield

icebox cakes

Simply Irresistible No-Bake Desserts

THE HARVARD COMMON PRESS BOSTON, MASSACHUSETTS

The Harvard Common Press
535 Albany Street
Boston, Massachusetts 02118
www.harvardcommonpress.com

Printed in China
Printed on acid-free paper

Library of Congress Cataloging-in-Publication Data
Chattman, Lauren.
   Icebox cakes : simply irresistible no-bake desserts / Lauren Chattman.
      p. cm.
   Includes index.
   ISBN 1-55832-344-9 (hardcover : alk. paper) — ISBN 1-55832-345-7
(pbk. : alk. paper)
1. Cake. 2. Cookery (Cold dishes) I. Title.
   TX771.C457 2007
   641.8'653—dc22

                                                    2006026170

ISBN-13: 978-1-55832-344-5 (hardcover); 978-1-55832-345-2 (paperback)
ISBN-10: 1-55832-344-9 (hardcover); 1-55832-345-7 (paperback)

Special bulk-order discounts are available on this and other Harvard
Common Press books. Companies and organizations may purchase books
for premiums or resale, or may arrange a custom edition, by contacting
the Marketing Director at the address above.

Book design by Night & Day Design
Photography by Duane Winfield
Food styling by Mariann Sauvion and Grady Best

10 9 8 7 6 5 4 3 2 1

Acknowledgments

Pam Hoenig came up with the "icebox" idea, and three books later
I sincerely thank her.

Thanks to everyone at The Harvard Common Press—Bruce Shaw,
Valerie Cimino, Jane Dornbusch, Virginia Downes, Pat Jalbert-Levine,
Betsy Young, Christine Alaimo, Howard Stelzer, Amy Etcheson,
Abby Collier, Janice Geary, Becca Hansen, and Megan Weireter.
Not only did they turn this manuscript into a book,
they enthusiastically tested recipes.

Thanks also to copyeditor Karen Levy for editorial fine-tuning.

The photos show how much fun I had making these cakes. Thanks
again to photographer Duane Winfield for knowing just how to present
them. Mariann Sauvion and Grady Best did a wonderful job of styling
the cakes for the photo shoot, and I'm so grateful to Night & Day
Design for a beautiful cover and interior design.

Thanks also to Angela Miller, for her advice and friendship.

My children have eaten a lot of icebox desserts in the past few years,
and are now coming up with recipe ideas of their own. Thank you,
Rose and Eve, for your contributions to this book.

And thanks to my husband, Jack Bishop. Your strong support allows
me to have so much fun in the kitchen.

contents

No-Bake Cakes

A couple of years ago, I wrote a book called *Icebox Desserts,* a follow-up to an earlier book called *Icebox Pies*. The idea behind both books is the same: It's possible to make delicious and beautiful desserts without turning on the oven. What's the trick, you ask? Use the refrigerator or freezer to finish a dessert. Chilling takes the place of baking. So instead of baking a pie, you fill a pie shell with a stovetop pudding and then refrigerate it until the filling is thick enough so that you can slice the pie. Or you assemble a trifle with store-bought pound cake, whipped cream, and fresh fruit and then refrigerate it to allow the components to combine and their flavors to meld.

The chapter on cakes in *Icebox Desserts* was my hands-down favorite. With no worries about baking, I could get right to the fun part: assembling and decorating the cake. So I explored some of the many possibilities: I layered Devil Dogs snack cakes with ice cream in a loaf pan and frosted it with whipped cream. I made a bûche de Noël not, as pastry bibles instruct, with a labor-intensive jelly roll, but by sticking together a box of chocolate wafer cookies with peppermint candy mousse and then disguising it as a log with strategically applied cocoa whipped cream. My no-bake berry cheesecake was a wonder of simplicity. Instead of fussing with water baths and temperamental filling, I thickened my cream cheese filling with unflavored gelatin, stuck the cake in the refrigerator, and removed it a few hours later without stress.

I had many more ideas for icebox cakes than space would allow, so I filed them away for future reference. I hoped I'd be allowed to return to the icebox well one more time, to fully explore the possibilities. Sure enough, my editor at The Harvard Common Press called one day to see if I'd like to expand that chapter into a book. So here it is, a collection of more than 50 new recipes for no-bake cakes that are fun to make and satisfying to eat.

What does a no-bake cake recipe look like? The variety may surprise you. But I'll tell you what each and every one *doesn't* contain. It's that deceptively simple item in the ingredients list that looks something like this: "2 yellow cake layers,

cooled and split (page 47)." Turn to page 47 and you get an intimidating page or two of instructions about making the cake layers before you can actually put the whole thing together. The recipes in this book, in contrast, skip that first forbidding step, because they use a variety of cake layer substitutes, or no cake layers at all. They're perfect for inexperienced bakers who nonetheless want to feel the thrill of producing a picture-perfect, great-tasting cake. But there's also a place for icebox cake in an experienced baker's repertoire. I am living proof of this. I'll never give up baking from scratch, but when I want to make a cake with a gratifyingly large fun-to-work ratio, maybe a S'mores Ice Cream Terrine (page 79) for a summer barbecue or a Valentine's Day Passion Fruit Icebox Cake (page 33) molded in a pretty heart-shaped pan, I turn to these recipes.

What in the World Is a No-Bake Cake?

"No-bake cake" may sound like an oxymoron, but the recipes in this book demonstrate otherwise. It is entirely possible to create a surprisingly wide range of cakes without turning on the oven. In the following pages, here is what you will find:

Chapter 1, Icebox Classics, is a collection of recipes using the classic cake layer substitutes: chocolate wafer cookies, sponge-type ladyfingers, and pound cake. These come in all shapes, from the classic log made with chocolate wafer cookies sandwiched with whipped cream to layer cakes bursting with berries and covered with cream cheese frosting to impressive bombes made by lining a bowl with slices of pound cake and filling the center with a delectable mousse.

In chapter 2, Raiding the Lunchbox, snack cakes beloved by children everywhere take the place of homemade cake layers, with impressive results. The pretty swirls of chocolate cake and cream in Black Forest Icebox Cake (page 49) come courtesy of Drake's Yodels. Twinkie Tiramisu (page 56) tastes surprisingly authentic. But you shouldn't really be surprised. Traditional tiramisu is made with ladyfingers, and, after all, Twinkies are nothing more than creme-filled sponge ladyfingers.

I wanted the cakes in chapter 3, Ice Cream Cakes for Every Taste, to demonstrate the versatility of store-bought ice cream. Everyone has a favorite way to dress up a favorite ice cream flavor, and here I show you a few of my own: pistachio ice cream layered with apricot ice cream (plain vanilla, mixed with some apricot preserves; page 71), a lemon and blueberry ice cream terrine (see page 84), and a spectacular terrine made with mango and raspberry sorbets and served with a decadent chocolate-coconut sauce (see page 81). In some of these recipes, you *will* find instructions to turn on the oven, but only for a few minutes, to crisp up the simple cookie crumb crusts that will hold layers of ice cream, caramel or hot fudge sauce, and lots of other good stuff.

Chapter 4, Easy and Elegant Terrines, focuses on frozen desserts for grown-up tastes. Triple Chocolate Mousse Terrine (page 95) is more refined than an ice cream cake, but just as entertaining, with its bands of dark, milk, and white chocolate frozen mousses. Rum-Pineapple Terrine (page 105) is made by folding together rich rum sabayon with some crushed pineapple and whipped cream. It's the kind of dessert that transports you to the tropics with one look and one bite.

The no-bake cheesecakes in chapter 5, No-Bake, No-Fail Cheesecakes, demonstrate that cream cheese is an excellent medium for a variety of favorite dessert flavors: lemon-blackberry, chocolate–peanut butter, maple syrup, and cappuccino. As with some of the ice cream cakes, these have cookie crumb crusts that do need to crisp up in the oven. But once the crusts are cooled, that's it. Fillings thickened with gelatin set up beautifully in the refrigerator, and the cakes themselves will keep, covered with plastic wrap, for up to a week, so you can enjoy them by the slice.

I didn't want to end the book without a few recipes for scaled-down icebox cakes. Chapter 6, Icebox Miniatures, is a collection of cupcakes and other single-serving icebox cakes with a charm all their own. I love to serve these little desserts and then sit back and listen to everyone exclaim over their cuteness.

Chill Out

Every single cake in this book must be refrigerated or frozen before it will be ready for serving. Wrap your cakes in plastic wrap as directed so that they don't absorb odors from the refrigerator or develop unsightly freezer burn.

Chilling times vary from recipe to recipe, but most cakes require at least 3 hours to set up properly. Individual recipes note how long a cake will keep. Some will begin to shed moisture quickly and are best served on the day they are made. Some may be wrapped in plastic wrap and frozen for a week or two with no diminishment in quality. Follow the chilling directions carefully, just as you would follow baking directions when baking a cake. In general, chilling is a more forgiving way of finishing a cake than baking is. An extra few minutes in the refrigerator won't ruin a cake the way an extra few minutes in the oven will. But quality will suffer if a cake isn't chilled long enough or is left to chill too long.

A few things to keep in mind when slicing icebox cakes: Ice cream cakes should soften up a little bit on the countertop before they are sliced. Not only is cutting through a rock-hard cake difficult, but it also can be dangerous if a sharp knife slips from your hands while you attempt to saw through an icy block of frozen mousse. Refrigerated cakes can be sliced straight from the refrigerator. For the neatest, best-looking slices, wipe your knife with a paper towel between cuts.

This way, the layers of cake and filling that you've so carefully arranged will be perfectly visible, not streaked with frosting from the previous slice.

Ingredients for Icebox Cakes

All of the icebox cakes in this book are chilled so that they'll hold their shape. So it shouldn't be surprising that no matter how different they are in taste, texture, and appearance, they use the same refrigerator-friendly staple ingredients to help them accomplish this goal. Here is a list of common icebox items, some of which are rarely seen in conventional cake recipes, to give you an idea of what you will need to buy.

Candy: Icebox cakes are all about fun, and what's more fun than a candy bar? I'll often use a layer of chopped Heath Bars or Butterfingers to add texture to a cake. Chopped candy bars also make a fun and quick garnish: Press them into the sides of a cake or sprinkle them on top in place of nonpareils or chopped nuts.

Chocolate: Not only does chocolate add flavor to icebox cakes, it has thickening properties as well. For icebox cakes I like to use premium brands such as Lindt, Callebaut, Valrhona, and Ghirardelli. When melted, they are creamy and smooth, not grainy like inexpensive baking chocolate, which I save for brownie baking and the like.

Cookies and cookie crumbs: To make the desserts in this book, I rely on a long list of cookies from the supermarket: Nabisco Famous

Chocolate Wafers, graham crackers, vanilla wafers, gingersnaps, ladyfingers, shortbreads, creme-filled wafers, Nutter Butters, and amaretti. Crushed cookies make crisp crusts for ice cream cakes and no-bake cheesecakes. When whole cookies are layered with whipped cream, pudding, or mousse, they absorb some moisture from these filling ingredients, becoming cake-like layers. Most of these cookies have extraordinarily long shelf lives, but do store cookie leftovers in a zipper-lock plastic bag to keep out moisture, so that they'll be fresh-tasting when you need them for a new creation.

Cornstarch: Use this thickener to give body to puddings and pastry creams. To prevent lumps from forming, be sure to dissolve it in a liquid before whisking it into the other ingredients.

Cream cheese: The bagel's best friend is also a key ingredient in icebox cheesecakes and other cakes. Any brand of cream cheese should be fine, but use only full-fat cream cheese. Low-fat and nonfat versions taste more like paste than cheese. For the smoothest fillings, be sure to bring cream cheese to room temperature before using it.

Eggs: Eggs thicken and enrich many icebox cake fillings. All of the recipes in this book were tested with large eggs. Although in most cases they are cooked to a safe temperature of 160°F, there are a couple of recipes that call for raw eggs. Because of the remote but dangerous possibility that raw eggs carry salmonella, they should not be used in food to be consumed by children, pregnant women, elderly people, or anyone in poor health or with a compromised immune system.

Gelatin: A flavorless, colorless thickener, gelatin comes as a powder in individual envelopes and must be dissolved in cold water, then melted over hot water (if it's not going to be added to a hot mixture) before being used to turn a liquid into a solid.

Heavy cream: A book on icebox cakes is unimaginable without this key ingredient. To whip cream to its highest volume, chill the cream, bowl, and beaters before whipping. Whip the cream as directed, either until it holds soft peaks (when the whisk or beater is lifted up from the cream and the cream forms a point that gently flops over) or until it holds stiff peaks (the point will stand upright). Properly whipped cream is also smooth and shiny. Underwhipping will rob your cake of beautiful height and delicious lightness. But take care not to overwhip it. Overwhipped cream forms lumps and ultimately separates into liquid and blobs of butterfat. If you turn your back on the mixer and this happens, you'll have to start all over again with fresh cream.

Ice cream and sorbet: In my opinion, premium brands such as Häagen-Dazs and Ben & Jerry's have the most butterfat and the freshest flavors, making for the richest, best-tasting cakes.

Be guided by your own taste. If you enjoy it in a cone, you will like it just as much or even more in a cake. Follow the softening tips and guidelines in the recipes. It is impossible to spread rock-hard ice cream into smooth cake layers.

Liqueurs, wines, and spirits: In some recipes, the addition of a small amount of these gives a grown-up flavor to an icebox cake. Buy miniature bottles at the liquor store if you don't think you'll drink the leftovers of a bigger bottle of Kahlúa or crème de menthe.

Nuts and seeds: Chopped nuts add richness and texture to crumb crusts. I also press them into the sides of cakes for a quick and pretty decoration. Praline candy made with sesame seeds, pumpkin seeds, sliced almonds, walnuts, or pecans can also be ground up and used as a layering ingredient, or broken into shards to make a dramatic garnish for an icebox cake. Store unused nuts and seeds in zipper-lock plastic bags in the freezer to preserve their freshness.

Pound cake: I've always liked Sara Lee's frozen pound cake, which I use straight from the freezer. Once sliced, it defrosts very quickly. For this book, I also tried Entenmann's, a regional brand of freshly baked cake sold near the bread in the supermarket, and I found it to be delicious. I refrigerate it until I'm going to use it, and then freeze any scraps in a zipper-lock plastic bag. I have also included a recipe for Homemade Pound Cake (page 15), in case you're feeling ambitious.

Snack cakes: If sliced pound cake and ladyfingers can be used in place of home-baked cake layers, why shouldn't Twinkies, Devil Dogs, and mini doughnuts work as well? I had a lot of fun trying to figure out the best ways to use snack cakes that I usually pack in a lunch box to create great-looking icebox desserts. If you've ever bought a box of any of these, then you shouldn't be above trying one of the recipes in chapter 2.

Equipment for Icebox Cakes

If you have baked at all in the past, you probably have most of the equipment you need to make any of the cakes in this book. Here's a list of the basics, most of which are inexpensive and available at most housewares shops and in the baking aisle of many supermarkets.

Baking pans and sheets: A 9-inch springform pan, a 9½ x 4 x 3-inch loaf pan, a 12-cup muffin tin, and a rimmed baking sheet are all you need to make these cakes. Because you won't actually be baking in any of these, don't worry if yours are old, cheap, and/or flimsy. That aluminum muffin tin might leave you with scorched muffins every time, but because you are using it only for its shape in these recipes, the quality of the metal and the finish won't affect the quality of the dessert.

Mixing bowls: I regularly use two sets of nesting mixing bowls, one metal and one glass, for a variety of icebox tasks: organizing ingredients, softening gelatin, improvising a double boiler, and cooling a bowl of hot filling by placing it in a bowl of ice water. Sometimes I'll even assemble a domed cake inside a mixing bowl.

Electric mixer: I use a heavy-duty KitchenAid mixer, but a handheld mixer will work just as well for whipping heavy cream, beating cream cheese, and the like.

Food processor: Because I have one, I use it regularly to grind cookies and nuts, but these jobs can be accomplished just as well by hand.

Measuring cups and spoons: For best results with these recipes, measure accurately and carefully with glass or clear plastic "liquid" measuring cups for liquid ingredients and plastic or metal "dry" measuring cups for large quantities of dry ingredients. For small quantities, use measuring spoons. Fill cups and spoons completely, and level off dry ingredients with a knife for accurate measurements.

Paper liners for muffin tins: Use regular-size paper liners to line muffin tins before assembling icebox cupcakes. The smaller size liners, which fit in mini-muffin tins, are good for making icebox petit fours.

Plastic wrap: I routinely line loaf pans and bowls with a double layer of plastic wrap before assembling cakes inside of them. Then, when I'm ready to unmold the cakes, I just tug at the overhanging edges of the wrap to loosen the cake, invert it onto a serving platter, and peel away the plastic. Plastic wrap is also essential for preserving the freshness of icebox cakes kept in the refrigerator or freezer for longer than an hour or two.

Saucepans: Good-quality saucepans in small, medium, and large sizes are a must if you don't want your pudding and custard cake fillings to scorch. Heavy anodized aluminum or stainless-steel pans from All-Clad are my first choice.

Spatulas: Spatulas are key tools for making beautiful icebox cakes. Flexible rubber spatulas scrape fillings from bowls and fold whipped cream together with other ingredients. A small metal offset spatula or spreader is essential for spreading fillings and frostings smoothly. I also use an extra-wide spatula or turner to loosen frozen cakes from baking sheets and to transfer cakes safely from baking sheets to serving platters.

Strainer: A fine-mesh strainer will remove lumps from pastry cream and other custards.

Wire whisk: Stirring pastry cream, pudding, or custard with a whisk is the best way to break up any lumps and ensure the smoothest result.

Homemade Pound Cake

Makes one 1-pound loaf

This recipe makes more than enough cake to use in any of the recipes in this book. Snack on leftovers, or place them in a zipper-lock plastic bag and freeze, adding new leftovers as you bake fresh pound cakes, until you have enough to make another icebox cake.

4 large eggs, at room temperature

2 teaspoons pure vanilla extract

1½ cups unbleached all-purpose flour

¾ teaspoon baking powder

¼ teaspoon salt

1 cup (2 sticks) unsalted butter, softened

1¼ cups sugar

1. Preheat the oven to 325°F. Coat the inside of a 9½ x 4 x 3-inch loaf pan with nonstick cooking spray and dust it with flour, knocking out any extra flour.

2. Combine the eggs and vanilla extract in a glass measuring cup and lightly beat. Combine the flour, baking powder, and salt in a medium-size mixing bowl.

3. Combine the butter and sugar in a large mixing bowl and cream with an electric mixer on medium-high speed until fluffy, about 3 minutes, scraping down the sides of the bowl once or twice as necessary.

4. With the mixer on medium-low speed, pour the egg mixture into the bowl in a slow stream, stopping the mixer once or twice to scrape down the sides.

5. Turn the mixer to low speed and add the flour mixture, ½ cup at a time, scraping down the sides of the bowl after each addition. After the last addition, mix for 30 seconds on medium speed.

6. Scrape the batter into the prepared pan and smooth the top with a rubber spatula. Bake the cake until it is golden and a toothpick inserted into the center comes out clean, about 1 hour and 15 minutes. Let the cake cool in the pan for about 5 minutes, then remove it by inverting it onto a wire rack. Turn the cake right side up to cool completely. Homemade Pound Cake will keep, wrapped in plastic wrap, at room temperature for up to 3 days, refrigerated for up to 1 week, or frozen for up to 1 month.

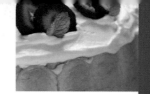
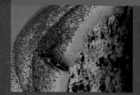

CHAPTER 1

icebox classics

Early in this project, when I surveyed the recipes already out there for icebox cakes, three ingredients cropped up regularly: Nabisco Famous Chocolate Wafers, ladyfingers, and pound cake. So I decided to begin my book with cakes made with these classic cake builders.

As it turns out, there are quite a lot of unusual and exciting desserts you can make using any one of these three items as a base. The recipe on the back of the box of Nabisco Famous Chocolate Wafers was the inspiration for the first four cakes in this chapter. When sandwiched with whipped cream and allowed to stand in the refrigerator or freezer, the cookies absorb some of the cream's moisture, becoming soft and a little puffy, more like cake. Traditionally, the cookies and cream are lined up in a log shape and then slathered with more cream. But you can also shape them into a ring (White Chocolate and Orange Icebox Ring, page 23) or layer them inside a springform pan (Fresh Raspberry Icebox Cake, page 25), lining the sides of the pan with more wafer cookies to make a fun and graphic polka dot pattern.

At the supermarket I was confronted with two types of ladyfingers: American-style sponge cake cookies and the crispier Savoiardi biscuits made in Italy and used in traditional tiramisu. I quickly discovered the sponge cake cookies were the better choice for these desserts, keeping their shape as they absorbed some of the moisture from the fillings. The Italian biscuits remained too crunchy for eating enjoyment, even after many hours in the refrigerator. So I used the sponge cake cookies to make a creamy strawberry cake (see page 27) and a decadent chocolate-and-toffee cake (see page 30). Both get pudding-like richness from homemade pastry cream.

All-butter pound cake from the freezer case is a boon for nonbakers who nonetheless want to produce impressive cakes. *Zuccotto* and Southern Belle (pages 36 and 39) are assembled in bowls and then unmolded, becoming impressive (or impressively silly in the case of the Southern Belle) bombes. The Winter Pudding Cake (page 41) contains berries from the freezer case layered with that same pound cake, for times when you're longing for juicy berry flavor in the middle of February. Instead of layering the fruit with slices of white bread (as the rather austere summer version of this dessert does), I use buttery pound cake, which holds its own against the fruit and cream.

The final recipe in this chapter doesn't use chocolate cookies, ladyfingers, or pound cake. It's a delectably light mousse cake made with the always classic rice pudding, so I hope I put it right where it belongs.

festive icebox cake

Serves 10

Here's the classic, updated with a frosting of cocoa whipped cream and a sprinkling of rainbow nonpareils for color. Resist the urge to serve this right away. To achieve a pleasingly soft consistency, this cake must be frozen for at least 6 hours.

2¾ cups heavy cream, chilled

½ cup confectioners' sugar

1 teaspoon pure vanilla extract

36 Nabisco Famous Chocolate Wafers

2 tablespoons unsweetened cocoa powder, Dutch-processed or natural, sifted

2 tablespoons rainbow nonpareils or sprinkles

continued from page 19

1. Whip 1½ cups of the cream, ¼ cup of the confectioners' sugar, and the vanilla extract together in a large bowl with an electric mixer until soft peaks form.

2. Stack 6 cookies on top of each other, spreading about 1 tablespoon of the whipped cream mixture on top of each wafer, and topping the final wafer in the stack with some whipped cream. Repeat until you have 6 stacks of 6 wafers.

3. Lay the cookie stacks on their sides, next to each other, on a rimmed baking sheet to make a 14-inch log. Wrap the log in plastic wrap and freeze until firm, at least 6 hours and up to 1 week.

4. When ready to continue, combine the remaining 1¼ cups heavy cream, the remaining ¼ cup confectioners' sugar, and the cocoa powder in a medium-size bowl and whip with the mixer until it holds stiff peaks.

5. Spread the cocoa whipped cream evenly over the log. Sprinkle with the nonpareils. Loosen the cake from the baking sheet with a wide spatula. Using two wide spatulas, carefully transfer it to a long serving platter. Let the cake stand at room temperature for 15 to 20 minutes before slicing and serving.

tiramisu icebox cake

Serves 10

This icebox cake incorporates the flavors of tiramisu—tangy mascarpone and espresso. A dusting of cocoa powder finishes off the cake, just as it finishes off classic tiramisu, and adds intense chocolate flavor. Mascarpone is a wonderfully rich Italian-style cream cheese, available at most supermarkets and Italian and gourmet grocery stores. Warm Chocolate Sauce (page 25) is the perfect accompaniment if you are a mocha fan.

2 cups heavy cream, chilled

½ cup confectioners' sugar

1 tablespoon instant espresso powder

1 teaspoon pure vanilla extract

One 8-ounce container mascarpone cheese, softened

36 Nabisco Famous Chocolate Wafers

2 tablespoons unsweetened cocoa powder, Dutch-processed or natural, sifted

1 recipe Warm Chocolate Sauce (optional; page 25)

continued from page 21

1. Whip the cream, confectioners' sugar, espresso powder, and vanilla extract together in a large bowl with an electric mixer until soft peaks form. Add the softened mascarpone and continue to whip until smooth, scraping down the sides of the bowl once or twice as necessary.

2. Stack 6 cookies on top of each other, spreading about 1 tablespoon of the whipped cream mixture on top of each wafer, and topping the final wafer in the stack with some whipped cream. Repeat until you have 6 stacks of 6 wafers.

3. Lay the cookie stacks on their sides, next to each other, on a rimmed baking sheet to make a 14-inch log. Use a small offset spatula to smooth the remaining whipped cream mixture over the log. Cover with plastic wrap and refrigerate until firm, 4 to 6 hours.

4. Just before serving, sift the cocoa powder over the cake. Loosen the cake from the baking sheet with a wide spatula. Using two wide spatulas, carefully transfer it to a long serving platter. Serve with the Warm Chocolate Sauce, if desired.

white chocolate and orange icebox ring

Serves 10

White chocolate and orange zest added to the whipped cream filling give this cake richness and bright flavor. The chopped bittersweet chocolate pressed into the sides is a pretty garnish and adds bracing bitterness to the sweet confection. You could make this cake in the usual log shape, but it's just as easy to shape it into a ring, using the sides of a springform pan as your guide. Bring the heavy cream to room temperature before whipping, so that when you add the melted chocolate it won't solidify before becoming incorporated.

7 ounces best-quality white chocolate, finely chopped

3 cups heavy cream, at room temperature

6 tablespoons confectioners' sugar

1½ teaspoons grated orange zest

2 tablespoons Grand Marnier or other orange liqueur

36 Nabisco Famous Chocolate Wafers

4 ounces bittersweet chocolate, finely chopped

continued from page 23

1. Put 2 inches of water in a medium-size saucepan and bring to a bare simmer. Combine the chocolate and 1 cup of the heavy cream in a stainless-steel bowl big enough to rest on top of the saucepan. Place the bowl over the simmering water, making sure that the bottom of the bowl doesn't touch the water. Heat, whisking occasionally, until the chocolate is completely melted. Remove the bowl from the heat and let cool slightly.

2. Whip the remaining 2 cups cream, the confectioners' sugar, orange zest, and Grand Marnier in a large bowl with an electric mixer until soft peaks form. With the mixer still running, scrape the chocolate mixture into the bowl all at once and continue to whip until smooth.

3. Stack 6 cookies on top of each other, spreading about 1 tablespoon of the whipped cream mixture on top of each wafer, and topping the final wafer in the stack with whipped cream. Repeat until you have 6 stacks of 6 wafers. Place the remaining whipped cream mixture in the refrigerator.

4. Place the outside ring of a 9-inch springform pan, without the bottom, on a serving platter. Lay the cookie stacks on their sides, end to end, against the inside of the pan to form a ring with an open center. Place in the freezer for about 30 minutes to firm up.

5. Remove the cake from the freezer. Run a sharp paring knife around the edges of the cake and release the pan sides from it. Smooth the remaining whipped cream mixture over the cake. Cover with plastic wrap and freeze for at least 6 hours and up to 1 week.

6. About 15 minutes before serving, remove the cake from the freezer and press the chopped bittersweet chocolate into the sides of the cake.

fresh raspberry icebox cake with warm chocolate sauce

Anyone who knows me knows my love of polka dots. The wafer cookies placed along the sides of the springform pan make big beautiful dots for this simple dessert.

Serves 10

2 cups heavy cream, chilled

½ cup confectioners' sugar

1 teaspoon pure vanilla extract

36 Nabisco Famous Chocolate Wafers

4 cups fresh raspberries

Warm Chocolate Sauce

12 ounces bittersweet chocolate, finely chopped

6 tablespoons water

1½ tablespoons raspberry liqueur (optional)

continued from page 25

1. Whip the cream, confectioners' sugar, and vanilla extract together in a large bowl with an electric mixer until soft peaks form.

2. Arrange 12 cookies in a single layer on the bottom of a 9-inch springform pan. Arrange 1½ cups of the raspberries on top of the cookies. Scrape two-thirds of the whipped cream over the raspberries and smooth with a small offset spatula.

3. Stand 12 cookies against the sides of the pan all the way around, pushing them into the whipped cream so they stay upright.

4. Arrange the remaining 12 cookies on top of the whipped cream. Spread the remaining one-third of the whipped cream evenly over the cookies. Arrange 1½ cups of the raspberries on top of the whipped cream. Cover the pan with plastic wrap and refrigerate for at least 4 hours and up to 1 day.

5. To make the sauce, put 2 inches of water in a medium-size saucepan and bring to a bare simmer. Combine the chocolate and 6 tablespoons water in a stainless-steel bowl big enough to rest on top of the saucepan and place the bowl over the simmering water, making sure that the water doesn't touch the bottom of the bowl. Heat the chocolate, whisking occasionally, until it is completely melted. Turn off the heat. Stir in the liqueur if you are using it. (Warm Chocolate Sauce will keep, refrigerated in an airtight container, for up to 2 days. Reheat in the microwave for 1½ minutes or over a pot of simmering water.)

6. Just before serving, release the sides of the springform pan from the cake and arrange the remaining 1 cup raspberries around the top edge. Slice and serve with the sauce on the side.

strawberries and cream icebox cake

This cake has all of the components of a classic trifle, but because it is contained by a ring of ladyfingers it has a tailored, formal look. Be aware that the cake is very soft, and pieces will be a little messy-looking on serving plates. So give your guests a chance to admire your handiwork before you serve it up.

Serves 10

Vanilla Pastry Cream

2 cups half-and-half

½ cup granulated sugar

Pinch of salt

2 large eggs

1 large egg yolk

2½ tablespoons cornstarch

¼ cup (½ stick) unsalted butter, cut into 4 pieces

1 teaspoon pure vanilla extract

62 sponge cake–type ladyfingers (two and a half 3-ounce packages)

2 cups heavy cream, chilled

¼ cup confectioners' sugar

1 teaspoon pure vanilla extract

2 pints fresh strawberries, stemmed and thinly sliced

continued from page 27

1. To make the pastry cream, combine the half-and-half, 6 tablespoons of the granulated sugar, and the salt in a large heavy saucepan and bring to a simmer over medium heat, whisking frequently.

2. Meanwhile, in a large bowl, whisk together the eggs, egg yolk, cornstarch, and the remaining 2 tablespoons granulated sugar until pale yellow and smooth, about 1 minute.

3. When the half-and-half mixture is simmering, remove from the heat and gradually whisk it into the egg mixture, going slowly and whisking constantly so as not to curdle the eggs. Return the mixture to the pan and cook over medium heat, whisking constantly, just until a few bubbles break through the surface and the mixture has thickened and is shiny, 1 to 2 minutes.

4. Remove from the heat and whisk in the butter, one piece at a time, and the vanilla extract. Pour through a fine-mesh strainer into a heatproof bowl and press plastic wrap directly onto the surface of the hot pastry cream to prevent a skin from forming. Refrigerate until well chilled, at least 3 hours and up to 2 days.

5. To assemble the cake, line the sides of a 9-inch springform pan with about 20 ladyfingers, standing them up side by side, rounded side out. Arrange 14 ladyfingers on the bottom of the pan to cover it.

6. Whip the cream, confectioners' sugar, and vanilla extract together in a large bowl with an electric mixer until soft peaks form. Reserve about 2 cups of the whipped cream, transferring it to a smaller bowl. Gently fold the pastry cream into the remaining whipped cream.

7. Spread half of the pastry cream mixture over the ladyfingers and smooth with a spatula. Arrange half of the strawberries in a single layer on top of the pastry cream. Arrange 14 ladyfingers over the strawberries. Smooth the remaining pastry cream mixture over the ladyfingers. Arrange the remaining strawberries over the cream. Top with the remaining 14 ladyfingers.

8. Smooth the reserved whipped cream over the last layer of ladyfingers. Cover the pan with plastic wrap and refrigerate until firm, at least 3 hours and up to 1 day.

9. Just before serving, release the sides of the springform pan from the cake.

chocolate and toffee cream cake

This luscious chocolate pudding–filled cake gets just a little crunch from toffee bits layered throughout. Other candy bars with some crunch, such as Butterfingers, may be chopped up and substituted according to your taste.

Serves 10

Chocolate Pastry Cream

2 cups half-and-half

½ cup granulated sugar

3 tablespoons unsweetened cocoa powder, Dutch-processed or natural, sifted

Pinch of salt

2 large eggs

1 large egg yolk

2½ tablespoons cornstarch

2 tablespoons (¼ stick) unsalted butter, cut into 4 pieces

3 ounces bittersweet chocolate, finely chopped

1 teaspoon pure vanilla extract

62 sponge cake–type ladyfingers (two and a half 3-ounce packages)

2 cups heavy cream, chilled

¼ cup confectioners' sugar

1 teaspoon pure vanilla extract

1 cup Heath Milk Chocolate English Toffee Bits

1. To make the pastry cream, combine the half-and-half, 6 tablespoons of the granulated sugar, the cocoa powder, and the salt in a large heavy saucepan and bring to a simmer over medium heat, whisking frequently.

2. Meanwhile, in a large bowl, whisk together the eggs, egg yolk, cornstarch, and the remaining 2 tablespoons granulated sugar until pale yellow and smooth, about 1 minute.

3. When the half-and-half mixture is simmering, remove from the heat and gradually whisk it into the egg mixture, going slowly and whisking constantly so as not to curdle the eggs. Return the mixture to the pan and cook over medium heat, whisking constantly, just until a few bubbles break through the surface and the mixture has thickened and is shiny, 1 to 2 minutes.

4. Remove from the heat and whisk in the butter, one piece at a time, and then the chocolate and vanilla extract. Pour through a fine-mesh strainer into a heatproof bowl and press plastic wrap directly onto the surface of the hot pastry cream to prevent a skin from forming. Refrigerate until well chilled, at least 3 hours and up to 2 days.

5. To assemble the cake, line the sides of a 9-inch springform pan with about 20 ladyfingers, standing them up side by side, rounded side out. Arrange 14 ladyfingers on the bottom of the pan to cover it.

6. Whip the cream, confectioners' sugar, and vanilla extract together in a large bowl with an electric mixer until soft peaks form. Reserve about 2 cups of the whipped cream, transferring it to a smaller bowl. Gently fold the chocolate pastry cream into the remaining whipped cream.

7. Spread half of the pastry cream mixture over the ladyfingers and smooth with a spatula. Sprinkle ½ cup of the toffee bits over the pastry cream mixture. Arrange 14 ladyfingers over the toffee bits. Smooth the remaining pastry cream mixture over the ladyfingers. Sprinkle the remaining ½ cup toffee bits over the pastry cream. Top with the remaining 14 ladyfingers.

8. Smooth the reserved whipped cream over the last layer of ladyfingers. Cover the pan with plastic wrap and refrigerate until firm, at least 3 hours and up to 1 day.

9. Just before serving, release the sides of the springform pan from the cake.

A Few Ways to Use Chocolate Pastry Cream

Once you know how to make Chocolate Pastry Cream (page 30), you can use it to create many wonderful and simple desserts. Here are a few ideas:

✳ **Chocolate Cream Pound Cake:** Serve the chocolate pastry cream as an accompaniment to homemade or store-bought pound cake. Garnish with fresh pitted cherries.

✳ **Chocolate Mousse:** Fold it together with sweetened whipped cream for chocolate mousse.

✳ **Chocolate Pudding Tart:** Fill a chocolate cookie crumb tart or pie crust with the pastry cream, top with a layer of sweetened whipped cream, and cover with fresh raspberries.

✳ **Chocolate and Banana Parfaits:** Layer chocolate pastry cream in parfait glasses with bananas and whipped cream.

✳ **Chocolate and Strawberry Napoleons:** Cut store-bought puff pastry into small rectangles, bake, and construct quick Napoleons using the pastry cream and sliced strawberries. Dust with confectioners' sugar before serving.

valentine's day passion fruit icebox cake

When I worked in the pastry kitchen at a high-end restaurant, I tasted passion fruit for the first time and got hooked on its unique and exotic flavor. Chefs special-order passion fruit, but it can be hard for consumers to find in the produce section of the supermarket. So I was thrilled when I saw flash-frozen passion fruit puree from Goya in the frozen foods aisle. Made in a heart-shaped pan, this cake is a sweet Valentine's treat.

Serves 6

About 22 sponge cake–type ladyfingers

1 envelope unflavored gelatin

¼ cup cold water

1 cup frozen passion fruit puree, thawed

½ cup plus 3 tablespoons granulated sugar

1¼ cups heavy cream, chilled

1 cup fresh raspberries, for garnish

continued from page 33

Raspberry Sauce

One 12-ounce bag frozen raspberries, thawed

¼ cup confectioners' sugar, or more to taste

1 tablespoon freshly squeezed lemon juice, or more to taste

1. To make the cake, line a 9-inch heart-shaped cake pan with plastic wrap so there is at least 1 inch overhanging the top of the pan on all sides. Cut about 11 ladyfingers in half crosswise and stand them up side by side, rounded ends down and rounded sides out, along the sides of the pan.

2. Sprinkle the gelatin over the cold water in a small bowl and let soften for several minutes.

3. Combine the passion fruit puree and ½ cup of the granulated sugar in a small saucepan and cook over medium heat, stirring, until the mixture is warm and the sugar has dissolved. Whisk in the gelatin mixture and continue to whisk until the gelatin is completely dissolved. Scrape the passion fruit mixture into a bowl and place over a bowl of ice water, whisking occasionally, until it is cool and has begun to thicken but has not yet gelled.

4. In a large bowl, using an electric mixer, whip the heavy cream with the remaining 3 tablespoons granulated sugar until it holds soft peaks. Fold the passion fruit mixture into the whipped cream. Pour the mixture into the cake pan and smooth with a spatula. Cover the passion fruit mousse with a layer of ladyfingers, cutting them to fit where necessary. Cover with plastic wrap and freeze for at least 6 hours and up to 1 week.

5. To make the sauce, place the raspberries in a blender or the work bowl of a food processor and process until smooth. Push the puree through a fine-mesh strainer to remove the seeds. Stir in the confectioners' sugar and lemon juice. (Raspberry Sauce will keep, refrigerated in an airtight container, for up to 3 days, and in the freezer for up to 6 months.)

6. To unmold the cake, unwrap it and gently tug at the overhanging plastic lining the pan to loosen the cake. Place a serving platter over the pan, invert, and shake to release. Peel away the plastic wrap.

7. Let the cake stand at room temperature until thawed, about 1 hour. Garnish with fresh raspberries and serve with the sauce on the side.

zuccotto

*Tiramisu is not the only Italian icebox dessert.
The dome-shaped cake called* zuccotto *is another
wonderfully rich and simple import. Slices of pound
cake are used to line a bowl, and then the bowl is filled
with sweetened whipped cream, chocolate, and nuts.
The lemon zest and brandy give the dessert its Italian
flavor. You can slice and serve the cake straight from
the freezer, but I like to let it stand for 20 minutes so the
outer edges are soft while the inside has the texture of
ice cream or* semifreddo.

Serves 8

One 10- to 12-ounce store-bought
pound cake, or 1 recipe Homemade
Pound Cake (page 15)

¼ cup brandy

1½ cups heavy cream, chilled

⅓ cup confectioners' sugar

½ teaspoon pure vanilla extract

6 ounces milk chocolate, finely
chopped

5 ounces semisweet chocolate,
finely chopped

¾ cup blanched almonds, finely
chopped

1 teaspoon grated lemon zest

1 tablespoon unsweetened cocoa
powder, Dutch-processed or natural

continued from page 36

1. Line a 1½-quart bowl with a double layer of plastic wrap so it overhangs the sides by at least 1 inch. Cut the pound cake into ⅜-inch-thick slices, and then cut each slice diagonally in half.

2. Place 12 cake triangles on a work surface and brush with some of the brandy. Arrange the brandy-brushed slices inside the bowl, brandy side in, so that the points of the cake triangles meet at the bottom center of the bowl. Fit more triangles into the spaces near the top of the bowl so that the inside of the bowl is completely covered, reserving the remaining cake and trimming any extra cake that extends above the edge of the bowl.

3. Whip the cream, confectioners' sugar, and vanilla extract together in a large bowl with an electric mixer until soft peaks form. Fold in both chopped chocolates, the chopped almonds, and the lemon zest.

4. Spoon the whipped cream mixture into the cake-lined bowl and smooth with a spatula. Brush the remaining cake triangles with the remaining brandy and arrange them on top of the filling to completely cover it. Tightly cover the bowl with plastic wrap and freeze until firm, at least 6 hours and up to 1 week.

5. To unmold, remove the plastic from the top of the bowl. Gently tug at the overhanging plastic lining the bowl to loosen the cake. Place a serving platter over the bowl, invert, and shake to release. Peel away the plastic. Let stand on the platter for 20 minutes.

6. Just before serving, sift the cocoa powder over the cake. Slice and serve.

southern belle

Serves 12

*After I unmolded my Zuccotto (page 36), I realized
I had the perfect base for a cake my daughters had
always begged for but I'd been too lazy to try, a dome-
shaped extravaganza decorated to look like a girl in a
gigantic hoop skirt. Here, I make a nonalcoholic version
of Zuccotto, with chocolate mousse inside, and embed a
brand-new Barbie-type doll in the center. Barbie is tall,
so I had to use a deeper bowl than the one used in the
previous recipe. The bowl from my KitchenAid Classic
mixer, 4 quarts, was just right. I also had to slice the
cake thinner, to have enough to line the bigger bowl.
I frost the cake with whipped cream (tinted pink, of
course) to look like a big hoop skirt, decorating it with
as many frills as will fit. For a kids' birthday party,
serve slices of the cake with scoops of chocolate, vanilla,
or strawberry ice cream.*

One 10- to 12-ounce store-bought
pound cake, or 1 recipe Homemade
Pound Cake (page 15)

1 envelope unflavored gelatin

¼ cup cold water

12 ounces bittersweet chocolate,
finely chopped

4¼ cups heavy cream, chilled

¼ cup granulated sugar

2 tablespoons confectioners' sugar

Pink or red food coloring

1 new Barbie doll

continued from page 39

1. Line a 4-quart bowl with a double layer of plastic wrap so it overhangs the sides by at least 1 inch. Cut the pound cake into ¼-inch-thick slices, and then cut each slice diagonally in half.

2. Arrange the slices inside the bowl so that the points of the cake triangles meet at the bottom center of the bowl, leaving a 1-inch circle at the bottom of the bowl uncovered (this is where you will insert the doll). Fit more triangles into the spaces near the top of the bowl so that the inside of the bowl is completely covered, reserving any remaining cake and trimming any extra cake that extends above the edge of the bowl.

3. Sprinkle the gelatin over the cold water in a small bowl and let soften for several minutes.

4. Put 2 inches of water in a medium-size saucepan and bring to a bare simmer. Combine the chocolate and ¼ cup of the heavy cream in a stainless-steel bowl big enough to rest on top of the saucepan. Place the bowl over the simmering water, making sure that the bottom of the bowl doesn't touch the water. Heat, whisking occasionally, until the chocolate is completely melted. Whisk in the gelatin mixture and continue to whisk until smooth, about 1 minute. Set aside to cool for 5 minutes.

5. In a large mixing bowl, using an electric mixer, whip 2½ cups of the heavy cream and the granulated sugar together until the cream holds stiff peaks. Whisk the chocolate into the whipped cream until the two are just combined.

6. Spoon the whipped cream mixture into the cake-lined bowl and smooth with a spatula. It won't come to the top of the bowl. Arrange the cake pieces on top of the filling, using the leftover cake triangles if necessary, to cover it. Tightly cover the bowl with plastic wrap and refrigerate until firm, at least 6 hours and up to 1 day.

7. To unmold, remove the plastic from the top of the bowl. Gently tug at the overhanging plastic lining the bowl to loosen the cake. Place a serving platter over the bowl, invert, and shake to release. Peel away the plastic.

8. Remove the doll's clothes from the waist down and wrap the doll with one piece of plastic to cover it completely from the waist to the toes. Wrap another piece of plastic around it from its waist to the top of its head (you'll remove this piece before serving). Submerge it in the top center of the cake just up to the top of its legs.

9. Whip the remaining 1½ cups cream with the confectioners' sugar and a drop or two of food coloring until the cream just holds stiff peaks. Smooth a thin layer of the cream over the "skirt" and up to the doll's waist. If desired, stir a drop or two more of food coloring into the remaining whipped cream (this will give you a darker pink), and place in a pastry bag fitted with a large star tip. Pipe a row of stars around the base of the cake, and decorate the skirt with stars as desired. Refrigerate for up to 3 hours. Remove the plastic wrap from the doll's body and hair before serving.

winter pudding cake

Serves 10

This dessert was inspired by summer pudding, the layered cake made with fresh summer berries and slices of leftover bread. When I want something similar in the middle of the winter, I turn to flash-frozen fruit, and layer it in a springform pan with slices of pound cake and a rich mixture of cream cheese and whipped cream. The cake needs to sit in the refrigerator for 4 hours to soak up the juices of the berries, but it tastes even better after a full day, when the flavors and textures have had a chance to meld.

Two 12-ounce bags unsweetened frozen mixed berries

1 cup sugar

One 10- to 12-ounce store-bought pound cake, or 1 recipe Homemade Pound Cake (page 15)

8 ounces cream cheese, softened and cut into 8 pieces

1 teaspoon pure vanilla extract

1½ cups heavy cream, chilled

continued from page 41

1. Combine the frozen berries and ½ cup of the sugar in a medium-size saucepan and cook over medium heat, stirring often, until the mixture resembles a loose jam, 12 to 15 minutes. Transfer to a bowl to cool completely.

2. Cut the pound cake into ⅓-inch-thick slices. Line the bottom of a 9-inch springform pan with cake slices, cutting them where necessary to cover the bottom of the pan completely. Set aside the remaining slices.

3. In a large bowl, using an electric mixer, beat together the cream cheese, the remaining ½ cup sugar, and the vanilla extract until smooth.

4. In a medium-size bowl, using an electric mixer, whip the heavy cream until it holds stiff peaks. Gently fold into the cream cheese mixture.

5. Spread half of the cooled fruit mixture over the pound cake. Smooth half of the cream cheese mixture over the fruit. Top with the remaining cake slices, cutting them to fit where necessary. Spread the remaining fruit over the cake. Smooth the remaining cream cheese mixture over the fruit.

6. Wrap the pan tightly in plastic and refrigerate for at least 4 hours and up to 1 day. Release the sides of the springform pan from the cake and serve.

rice pudding mousse cake with rum-raisin sauce

Serves 8

I love warm rice pudding, but I don't always love the way it seems to get heavier in the refrigerator. Here's one way to keep it light as you chill it—fold in some whipped cream, and add a little gelatin so that the lightened pudding doesn't collapse. I like to serve this cake with Rum-Raisin Sauce, because rice pudding just seems incomplete without the raisins, but in the summer I'll switch to Raspberry Sauce (page 35) or fresh sliced strawberries instead.

½ cup long-grain rice

Pinch of salt

3 cups milk

1 cinnamon stick, broken in half

¾ cup granulated sugar

1 envelope unflavored gelatin

¼ cup water

2 large eggs

1 teaspoon pure vanilla extract

1 cup heavy cream, chilled

Rum-Raisin Sauce

½ cup packed light brown sugar

¼ cup (½ stick) unsalted butter

½ cup heavy cream, chilled

Pinch of salt

½ cup raisins

2 tablespoons dark rum

1. To make the cake, spray a 6- to 8-cup ring mold with nonstick cooking spray.

2. Bring a large saucepan of water to a boil. Add the rice and salt, return to a boil, and continue to boil until the rice is almost tender, about 15 minutes. Drain well.

3. Combine the parboiled rice, the milk, cinnamon stick, and granulated sugar in the same saucepan (no need to wash it, just empty the water) Bring to a boil, reduce the heat to low, and simmer, uncovered, stirring frequently, until the rice is very tender and the mixture is somewhat reduced but still soupy, 20 to 25 minutes.

4. When the rice is almost cooked, sprinkle the gelatin over the ¼ cup water in a small bowl and let soften for 5 minutes.

5. Place the eggs and vanilla extract in a medium-size bowl and whisk to break up. Place ½ cup of the heavy cream in a small saucepan and heat until it is just about to boil. Slowly pour the hot cream into the bowl with the eggs and vanilla, whisking constantly.

6. Whisk the egg mixture into the pot with the rice mixture and simmer, stirring constantly, until the pudding begins to thicken, about 1 minute. Remove from the heat and whisk in the gelatin mixture. Transfer to a bowl and let cool to warm room temperature.

7. In a large bowl, using an electric mixer, whip the remaining ½ cup cream until it holds stiff peaks. Fold the cream into the rice pudding. Scrape the mousse into the prepared pan. Cover with plastic wrap and refrigerate for at least 6 hours and up to 1 day.

8. To make the sauce, combine the brown sugar, butter, heavy cream, and salt in a small saucepan and bring to a boil over medium-high heat, stirring to dissolve the sugar. Remove from the heat and stir in the raisins. Let stand 5 minutes and then stir in the rum. Let cool slightly. (Rum-Raisin Sauce can be made up to 2 days ahead and rewarmed on top of the stove or in the microwave.)

9. To unmold the cake, unwrap and dip the mold into a bowl of very hot tap water for 30 seconds. Place a serving platter over the top of the mold and invert, tapping to release. Slice and serve with the warm sauce on the side.

CHAPTER 2

raiding the lunchbox

using snack cakes to make spectacular icebox desserts

Ever since I built an icebox cake with Drake's Devil Dogs, ice cream, and maraschino cherries, and my family proclaimed me an evil genius, I have been itching to make other diabolically simple cakes using lunchbox snack cakes. The beauty of that first Devil Dog cake was that when I sliced it, the creme-filled chocolate cakes mimicked cake layers so very realistically. It looked better than my homemade cakes usually did. In fact, it looked downright professional.

So when I sat down to think about what else I could do with Devil Dogs and other snack cakes, I tried hard to come up with recipes that would take advantage of the looks of the cakes the way my first recipe did. I use Yodels in a Black Forest confection (page 49), arranging them so that when I slice the cake I get a fun spiral pattern in every piece. The tops of the Ring Dings in the Orange Bavarian Cake (page 53) become a cute polka dot decoration. The doughnuts in the Strawberry-Custard Doughnut Cake (page 58) create a fun take on a traditional strawberry shortcake ring made with biscuit dough.

I knew that Devil Dogs and Twinkies wouldn't be contributing homemade taste to my icebox cakes, so I compensated by using wholesome homemade fillings and frostings to boost the flavor quotient. Real whipped cream, fresh fruit, and top-quality bittersweet chocolate give these desserts an integrity that snack cakes, for all of their merits, just don't have. I'm delighted with the results. The icebox cakes in this chapter combine the convenience and fun of our kids' favorite lunchbox treats with the fresh flavor and goodness of simple homemade desserts.

black forest icebox cake

Serves 8

Cherries, chocolate, and heavy cream all figure prominently in traditional Black Forest cake recipes. Yodels snack cakes…well, not so much. But they work well here as cake layers, without any fuss at all. Be sure to cut the cake so that you slice through the Yodels the short way. Then you'll get a nice spiral pattern in each piece. To make a bakery-worthy decoration, take a block of chocolate and run a vegetable peeler over it, working directly over the cake. You'll get pretty chocolate curls with very little effort.

16 Yodels snack cakes

⅓ cup cherry preserves

12 ounces cream cheese, softened

½ cup confectioners' sugar

1 teaspoon pure vanilla extract

¾ cup heavy cream, chilled

1½-ounce block bittersweet or milk chocolate

continued from page 49

1. Line a baking sheet with parchment paper. Arrange 4 Yodels side by side on the sheet. Place another 4 Yodels next to the first four, end to end, so that you have a square layer consisting of 8 Yodels. Spread the preserves over the cakes in an even layer. Top with the remaining 8 snack cakes, arranging them the same way as the first layer. Press the cakes back into a neat square shape if they have shifted. Place the baking sheet in the freezer until the cakes are firm and the preserves are slightly hardened, about 1 hour.

2. Combine the cream cheese, confectioners' sugar, and vanilla extract in a medium-size mixing bowl. Using an electric mixer, beat until the cream cheese is very smooth and fluffy, scraping down the sides of the bowl several times as necessary. Add the cream and mix on low until incorporated. Scrape down the bowl and mix on medium-high until the mixture is thick but spreadable.

3. Remove the cake from the freezer and cover the top and sides with the cream cheese frosting. Lightly drape with plastic wrap and refrigerate until ready to serve, at least 3 hours and up to 1 day. Using two large spatulas, carefully transfer the cake to a serving platter. Let stand at room temperature for ½ hour before serving.

4. Just before serving, use a vegetable peeler to make chocolate curls, dropping them directly on top of the cake.

A Yodel by Any Other Name

My mom packed a Drake's Yodel, Devil Dog, Ring Ding, or Coffee Cake into my lunch box almost every day of my elementary school career. So imagine my shock when I discovered in college that my roommate from Texas had never even heard of them! Although Hostess Twinkies are available nationwide, some brands, like my beloved Drake's Cakes, can be tough to find in certain parts of the country. Here are the Hostess equivalents for the Drake's Cakes used in these recipes:

Drake's Yodels = Hostess Ho Hos
Drake's Devil Dogs = Hostess Suzy Q's
Drake's Ring Dings = Hostess Ding Dongs

If you grew up in the South and are devoted to Little Debbie snack cakes, you may substitute Little Debbie Swiss Cake Rolls for Yodels and Little Debbie Devil Cremes for Devil Dogs. Alas, Little Debbie doesn't make a Ring Ding/ Ding Dong equivalent.

If you grew up with Drake's Cakes and won't consider any substitutes, but are now living smack in the middle of Little Debbie territory, don't despair. Your childhood favorites are just a mouse click away. Www.hometown-treats.com carries everything in the Drake's repertoire, as well as snack cakes from Entenmann's and Tastykakes.

devil dog mousse cake

Serves 8

Since I made my first cake with Drake's Devil Dogs for Icebox Desserts (The Harvard Common Press, 2005), I've been fascinated by the possibilities that this and other snack cakes present for lazy bakers. Here, I layer the cakes with raspberry mousse and then cover the cake with milk chocolate ganache. Bring the ganache to warm room temperature so that it is loose enough to pour, but not so warm that it will melt the frozen mousse. The resulting dessert is a surprisingly elegant cake that will nonetheless delight the kids in your house.

1¼ teaspoons unflavored gelatin

2 tablespoons cold water

½ pint fresh raspberries, plus a few extra for garnish

6 tablespoons sugar

2 cups heavy cream, chilled

1 teaspoon pure vanilla extract

10 Devil Dogs snack cakes or other creme-filled devil's food cakes

10 ounces best-quality milk chocolate, finely chopped

2 tablespoons unsweetened cocoa powder, Dutch-processed or natural, sifted

continued from page 51

1. Line the bottom of a 9½ x 4 x 3-inch loaf pan with a rectangle of parchment paper.

2. Sprinkle the gelatin over the cold water in a small bowl and let soften for 2 minutes.

3. Combine the raspberries and sugar in a medium-size heavy saucepan and cook over medium-low heat, stirring a few times, until the sugar dissolves and the mixture is warm to the touch, 5 to 7 minutes. Stir in the gelatin mixture. Let cool to room temperature, stirring occasionally.

4. Combine 1 cup of the heavy cream and the vanilla extract in a large bowl and, using an electric mixer, whip until stiff peaks form. Gently fold in the cooled raspberry mixture, taking care not to deflate the cream.

5. Place 5 Devil Dogs widthwise in the bottom of the pan. Pour half of the mousse over the cakes, smoothing with a rubber spatula. Place the remaining 5 Devil Dogs over the mousse, and pour the remaining mousse on top of this layer of cakes, again smoothing with a rubber spatula. Tap the pan on the countertop a couple of times to ensure that the mousse sinks into every crevice. Cover with plastic wrap and freeze until firm, at least 3 hours and up to 1 day.

6. Combine the chocolate and cocoa in a large mixing bowl. Bring the remaining 1 cup heavy cream just to a boil in a small saucepan over medium-low heat. Pour the hot cream into the bowl and let the mixture stand for 5 minutes. Whisk until smooth. Pour the ganache through a strainer into a clean measuring cup. Cool to warm room temperature.

7. Remove the pan from the freezer. Run a sharp paring knife around the edge to loosen the cake. Place a wire rack over the pan and invert. Gently tap to release. Peel the parchment from the top of the cake.

8. Place the wire rack over a rimmed baking sheet. Pour the ganache over the top of the cake and let it drip down the sides, so that it completely covers the cake. Scoop up the ganache on the bottom of the baking sheet and smooth it over the cake to create a smooth chocolate surface. Let stand for 15 minutes to allow the ganache to firm up a bit. Use a wide spatula to transfer the cake to a serving platter. Garnish with raspberries, slice, and serve.

orange bavarian cake with chocolate polka dots

Since I love the flavors of chocolate and orange, I decided to combine chocolate snack cakes with orange Bavarian cream, keeping the round tops of the Ring Dings exposed for a polka dot effect.

Serves 8

10 Ring Dings snack cakes

1 envelope unflavored gelatin

¼ cup cold water

5 large egg yolks

½ cup plus 2 tablespoons sugar

1 cup half-and-half

Zest of 1 orange, removed in
1 thick strip with a vegetable peeler

1 or 2 drops orange food coloring

1½ cups heavy cream, chilled

continued from page 53

1. Line the bottom of a 9-inch springform pan with a circle of parchment paper. Arrange 8 of the Ring Dings, top sides down, on the bottom of the pan and at least ½ inch away from the edges. Coarsely chop the remaining 2 Ring Dings and set aside.

2. Sprinkle the gelatin over the cold water in a small bowl and let soften for 5 minutes. Whisk together the egg yolks and sugar in a large bowl. Fill another large bowl with ice water and set aside.

3. Bring the half-and-half and orange zest to a boil in a medium-size heavy saucepan. Pour the hot half-and-half into the yolk mixture in a slow stream, whisking constantly. Return the mixture to the pan and bring just to a boil. As soon as it begins to bubble, pour it through a fine-mesh strainer into a heatproof bowl. Whisk in the gelatin mixture. Return the orange zest to the mixture. Set the bowl over the bowl of ice water and let cool, whisking occasionally, until it is just beginning to thicken but is still liquidy. Stir in the orange food coloring so that the mixture is pale orange.

4. In a medium-size bowl, using an electric mixer, whip the heavy cream until it holds stiff peaks. Fold into the cooled Bavarian cream mixture.

5. Pour the Bavarian cream mixture into the pan and smooth with a spatula. Scatter the chopped Ring Dings over the cream in an even layer. Cover with plastic wrap and freeze until firm, at least 6 hours and up to 1 week.

6. Release the sides of the springform pan from the cake. Place a serving platter on top of the cake and invert. Remove the pan bottom and peel away the parchment circle. Let stand at room temperature for 15 minutes before serving.

twinkie tiramisu

Serves 8

As soon as I started working on this book, people came out of the woodwork exclaiming about "Twinkie Tiramisu." It turns out that there are many versions of tiramisu that substitute Twinkies for the more traditional ladyfingers. Twinkies are certainly easier to find in the supermarket than imported Savoiardi biscuits, the traditional tiramisu ingredient. To make the dessert even easier to shop for and less expensive, I substitute cream cheese for mascarpone. Use a box grater to grate the chocolate, and work quickly so that it doesn't melt in your hands.

¼ cup water

½ cup plus ⅓ cup sugar

¾ cup espresso or strong brewed coffee

¼ cup Kahlúa or other coffee-flavored liqueur (optional)

8 ounces cream cheese, softened

1 teaspoon pure vanilla extract

1½ cups heavy cream, chilled

10 Twinkies snack cakes, halved lengthwise

4 ounces semisweet chocolate, grated

1. Combine the water and ½ cup of the sugar in a small saucepan and bring to a boil, stirring to dissolve the sugar. Pour the syrup into a shallow heatproof bowl and stir in the espresso and Kahlúa, if you are using it. Let cool to room temperature.

2. Combine the cream cheese, the remaining ⅓ cup sugar, and the vanilla extract in a large bowl and, using an electric mixer, beat until smooth. In another large bowl, beat the heavy cream until it just holds stiff peaks. Gently fold the cream cheese mixture into the whipped cream, taking care not to deflate the cream.

3. One by one, dip 10 of the Twinkie halves into the syrup to moisten but not completely saturate them, and place them alongside each other in the bottom of a shallow 12 x 7-inch baking dish. Smooth half of the cream cheese mixture over the Twinkies. Sprinkle with half of the grated chocolate. Repeat with the remaining Twinkies, cream cheese mixture, and chocolate. Cover with plastic wrap and refrigerate for at least 6 hours and up to 1 day before serving.

strawberry-custard doughnut cake

Serves 8

One of my all-time favorite dessert recipes consists of shortcake dough portioned out on a cookie sheet in 8 mounds to create a ring that, once baked, is then split and filled with whipped cream and strawberries. I've substituted store-bought powdered sugar doughnuts for the biscuits and added some pastry cream to the whipped cream because I love the doughnut–pastry cream combination. (For an even simpler dessert, make 50 percent more whipped cream and leave the pastry cream out altogether.) I consider this an icebox dessert because the strawberries and cream are chilled before the cake is put together. But it's actually better to construct the cake close to serving time, so that the strawberries don't shed too much liquid, diluting the cream and making the doughnuts soggy.

2 pints strawberries, stemmed and sliced

½ cup sugar

½ teaspoon pure vanilla extract

1 cup heavy cream, chilled

½ recipe Vanilla Pastry Cream (page 27), well chilled

8 powdered sugar or plain doughnuts, split in half horizontally

1. Combine the strawberries, 6 tablespoons of the sugar, and the vanilla extract in a large bowl and refrigerate, stirring occasionally, until the sugar is dissolved and the berries have given off some juice, about 1 hour.

2. In a medium-size bowl, using an electric mixer, whip the heavy cream and the remaining 2 tablespoons sugar until it just holds stiff peaks. Gently fold the pastry cream into the whipped cream.

3. Arrange the bottom halves of the doughnuts in a ring on a large serving platter. Spoon some of the pastry cream mixture on top of each doughnut. Spoon the berries on top of each portion of pastry cream. Top with the remaining doughnut halves and serve.

CHAPTER 3

ice cream cakes for every taste

There's a special place in my heart for ice cream cakes. My birthday is in July, and I always had one at my parties growing up. Made with cookie crumbs and fudge sauce and slathered with whipped cream, the cake was always the perfect way to wind down after a hectic afternoon of Pin the Tail on the Donkey and Musical Chairs. My mother bought my cake at the local soft-serve shop, Carvel. Before starting to develop recipes for this chapter, I drove over to the Carvel in nearby Bridgehampton to do a little research. Like so many childhood treats revisited—Cap'n Crunch cereal and Swanson TV Dinners come to mind—the cake was a bit of a disappointment. I could do better myself, I thought. Here are the results of my efforts.

The chapter begins with round cakes put together in a springform pan. I like to start with a crumb crust, to give the cake some crunch. I just pat the crumbs onto the bottom of the pan, not up the sides, so that the pretty layers of ice cream and filling are visible when the cake is unmolded. Baking the crusts for 6 to 8 minutes in the oven will crisp up the crumbs so that they don't get soggy in the freezer.

The second half of the chapter contains recipes for ice cream terrines put together in a loaf pan. To unmold these, tug on the plastic wrap lining the pan, invert the terrine onto a platter, and peel away the plastic.

When putting together an ice cream cake, timing is everything. Let the ice cream you intend to use for your first layer sit on the countertop until it is soft but not yet melting. Depending on the room temperature and how cold your ice cream was to begin with, this will take 5 to 15 minutes. Check it every 5 minutes by inserting a knife into the center of the container and wiggling it. If you are in a hurry or your ice cream is particularly hard (I find this to be the case with ice cream that I buy at convenience stores; they must keep their freezers at –20°F!), you can microwave it for a few seconds. That way, the hard core will soften up before the ice cream on the outside begins to melt. Placing the ice cream in a bowl and mashing it with the back of a spoon will also make it more spreadable. A small metal spatula is great for smoothing the ice cream into an even layer. Once you've done the first layer, be sure to freeze it adequately before proceeding. If the previous layers are too soft, it will be difficult to pile new ones on top evenly. It goes without saying, but I'll say it anyway, that any dessert sauce should be cooled completely before it is sandwiched between layers of ice cream, or it will melt the ice cream.

Even if the kids are screaming for ice cream, exercise caution when slicing an ice cream cake. If the cake is very hard, it's better to wait a few minutes to let it soften up rather than risk injury from a knife that can't easily cut through the layers.

crowd-pleasing ice cream cake

This simple cake with vanilla and chocolate ice cream is sure to please everyone. The layer of chopped Heath Bars in the middle doesn't hurt, either. If you can find them, you may substitute 1 cup of Heath Milk Chocolate English Toffee Bits for the candy bars.

Serves 10

30 vanilla wafers (to yield about 1 cup crumbs)

3 tablespoons unsalted butter, melted

Four 1.4-ounce Heath Bars, finely chopped

2 pints vanilla ice cream, softened

2 pints chocolate ice cream

¾ cup heavy cream, chilled

2 tablespoons confectioners' sugar

1 teaspoon pure vanilla extract

1 cup fresh strawberries, stemmed and sliced

continued from page 62

1. Preheat the oven to 350°F. Place the vanilla wafers in the work bowl of a food processor and process until finely ground. Add the melted butter and pulse once or twice to moisten the crumbs. Press the mixture evenly into the bottom of a 9-inch springform pan, packing it tightly with your fingertips so it is even and compacted. Bake until crisp, 6 to 8 minutes. Let cool completely. (The crust may be wrapped in plastic wrap and frozen for up to 1 month.)

2. Place the Heath Bar pieces in the work bowl of the food processor (there's no need to clean the bowl) and process until finely ground. Set aside.

3. Spoon the vanilla ice cream into a large mixing bowl and mash with the back of a spoon until it is smooth but not yet melting. Scrape it into the pan and smooth it over the vanilla wafer crust with the spoon. Sprinkle the toffee bits over the ice cream. Pat lightly with your fingers to press them into the ice cream. Return the pan to the freezer to firm up, about 1 hour.

4. Spoon the chocolate ice cream into a large mixing bowl and mash with the back of a spoon until it is smooth but not yet melting. Scrape it into the pan and smooth it over the toffee bits with the spoon. Wrap the cake in plastic wrap and freeze until firm, at least 3 hours and up to 1 week.

5. In a large bowl, using an electric mixer, whip the heavy cream, confectioners' sugar, and vanilla extract together until the cream holds soft peaks. Remove the cake from the freezer and release the sides of the pan. Smooth the whipped cream over the top and return the cake to the freezer until the cream is firm, at least 1 hour and up to 6 hours.

6. Just before serving, arrange the sliced strawberries upright along the sides of the cake, gently pressing them into the sides.

Ice Cream Cakes to Please Any Crowd

There's always someone ready to make a liar out of me—the kid who doesn't like chocolate, the great aunt who is allergic to strawberries, the one person in town who doesn't like Heath Bar bits and happens to be coming to your house for a barbecue. If the Crowd-Pleasing Ice Cream Cake (page 62) doesn't exactly fit the bill, there are many ways to customize it so that it does. Here's a list of alternate crusts, ice creams, fillings, and decorations that you may use to make your cake please *your* crowd.

✳ **Crusts:** Either graham crackers (see Ginger and Caramel Ice Cream Cake, page 69) or Oreos (see Grasshopper Ice Cream Cake, page 67) should satisfy anyone who has an aversion to vanilla wafers.

✳ **Ice Cream:** Vanilla and chocolate too boring? Try coffee and cookie dough, rum raisin and coconut, peach and cherry vanilla, peanut butter cup and chocolate, pistachio and strawberry, or chocolate chocolate chip and cookies and cream.

✳ **Fillings:** Instead of using Heath Bars, sprinkle a thick layer of toasted sweetened flaked coconut, chopped peppermint patties, chopped KitKats, chopped Snickers bars, or chopped Butterfingers in between the ice cream layers. Or spread a favorite flavor of jam and some chopped nuts over the bottom layer of ice cream.

✳ **Decorations:** Instead of standing strawberry slices around the cake, press multicolored sprinkles, Sno-Cap nonpareil candies, M&M's, cookie crumbs, chopped nuts, grated chocolate, or more Heath Bar bits into the sides of the cake. For kids' birthday parties, I sometimes stick a dozen or so colorful lollipops in the frozen whipped cream for a lollipop forest effect, and then stand gummy bears around the edges of the cake in place of the strawberry slices.

grasshopper ice cream cake

Here's a simple dessert for anyone who loves chocolate and mint together. The Raspberry Sauce is optional (and nontraditional), but I love how the bright red fruit looks next to the green ice cream, and the way the acidity of the berries cuts the sweetness of the chocolate.

Serves 10

20 Oreos (to yield about 1½ cups crumbs)

2 tablespoons (¼ stick) unsalted butter, melted

8 ounces bittersweet chocolate, finely chopped

¼ cup water

1 tablespoon crème de menthe

2 pints mint chocolate chip ice cream

28 Andes Crème de Menthe Thins candies, coarsely chopped

1 recipe Raspberry Sauce (page 35)

continued from page 67

1. Preheat the oven to 350°F. Place the Oreos in the work bowl of a food processor and process until finely ground. Add the melted butter and pulse once or twice to moisten the crumbs. Press the mixture evenly into the bottom of a 9-inch spring-form pan, packing it tightly with your fingertips so it is even and compacted. Bake until crisp, 6 to 8 minutes. Let cool completely. (The crust may be wrapped in plastic wrap and frozen for up to 1 month.)

2. Bring 2 inches of water to a bare simmer in a medium-size saucepan. Combine the bittersweet chocolate and water in a stainless-steel bowl big enough to rest on top of the saucepan and set it over the pan, making sure it doesn't touch the water. Heat the chocolate, whisking occasionally, until completely melted. Remove from the heat and stir in the crème de menthe. Set aside to cool to room temperature.

3. Spoon the ice cream into a large mixing bowl and mash with the back of a spoon until it is smooth but not yet melting. Scrape it into the pan and smooth it over the crust with the spoon. Smooth the cooled chocolate sauce over the top of the cake and sprinkle with the chopped Andes mints. Wrap the pan in plastic wrap and freeze until firm, at least 6 hours and up to 1 week.

4. Release the sides of the pan from the cake before serving. Serve with the raspberry sauce on the side.

ginger and caramel ice cream cake

An abundant amount of chopped crystallized ginger stirred into vanilla ice cream gives this cake a spicy flavor and offsets the sweetness of the Caramel Sauce. Look for crystallized ginger in natural foods stores, where it is often sold in bulk. Make sure the ice cream has firmed up in the freezer and the sauce has cooled completely before spreading it on the cake. You don't want the warm sauce to melt the ice cream.

Serves 10

Graham Cracker Crust

11 whole graham crackers (to yield about 1⅓ cups crumbs)

5 tablespoons unsalted butter, melted

1 tablespoon light brown sugar

⅛ teaspoon salt

Caramel Sauce

¾ cup granulated sugar

¼ cup water

½ cup heavy cream, chilled

3 tablespoons dark rum (optional)

2 pints vanilla ice cream

½ cup finely chopped crystallized ginger

½ cup finely chopped pecans

continued from page 69

1. To make the crust, preheat the oven to 350°F. Place the graham crackers in the work bowl of a food processor and process until finely ground. Add the melted butter, brown sugar, and salt and pulse once or twice to moisten the crumbs. Press the mixture evenly into the bottom of a 9-inch springform pan, packing it tightly with your fingertips so it is even and compacted. Bake until crisp, 6 to 8 minutes. Let cool completely. (The crust may be wrapped in plastic wrap and frozen for up to 1 month.)

2. To make the sauce, combine the granulated sugar and water in a heavy small saucepan. Bring to a boil and continue to boil the mixture until it turns a light amber color. Do not stir. If part of the syrup is turning darker than the rest of the syrup, gently tilt the pan to even out the cooking.

3. When the syrup is a uniform amber color, stir in the heavy cream with a long-handled wooden spoon. Be careful, as the cream will bubble up. When the bubbling has subsided, stir in the rum, if you are using it. Transfer the sauce to a heatproof glass measuring cup and let cool completely. (Caramel Sauce will keep in an airtight container at room temperature for up to 1 week.)

4. To assemble the cake, spoon the ice cream and ginger into a large mixing bowl and mash with the back of a spoon until it is smooth but not yet melting. Scrape it into the pan and smooth it over the crust with the spoon. Freeze for about 30 minutes to firm up.

5. Smooth the cooled sauce over the top of the cake and sprinkle with the chopped pecans. Wrap the pan in plastic wrap and freeze until firm, at least 6 hours and up to 1 week.

6. Release the sides of the pan from the cake before serving.

pistachio and apricot ice cream cake

Serves 10

To me, this cake has an irresistible combination of *Mediterranean flavors. The pistachios and apricots, and the cardamom that spices the whipped cream, work together beautifully to create a surprisingly complex dessert, considering how simple it is to put together. For the crust, one box of shortbread cookies will do. There will be just enough cookie crumbs to lightly cover the bottom of the pan.*

Shortbread Crust

8 shortbread cookies, such as 1 box Walker's (to yield about 1 cup crumbs)

¼ cup shelled unsalted pistachio nuts

2 tablespoons (¼ stick) unsalted butter, melted

2 pints vanilla ice cream

½ cup apricot jam

2 pints pistachio ice cream

¾ cup heavy cream, chilled

2 tablespoons confectioners' sugar

¼ teaspoon ground cardamom

continued from page 71

1. To make the crust, preheat the oven to 350°F. Place the shortbread cookies and shelled pistachios in the work bowl of a food processor and process until finely ground. Add the melted butter and pulse once or twice to moisten the crumbs. Press the mixture evenly into the bottom of a 9-inch springform pan, packing it tightly with your fingertips so it is even and compacted. Bake until crisp, 6 to 8 minutes. Let cool completely. (The crust may be wrapped in plastic and frozen for up to 1 month.)

2. Spoon the vanilla ice cream into a large mixing bowl and add the apricot jam. Mash with the back of a spoon until the ice cream is smooth but not yet melting and the apricot jam is incorporated. Scrape half of it into the pan and smooth it over the crust with a small offset spatula. Place in the freezer to firm up, at least 15 minutes. Place the bowl with the remaining ice cream in the freezer until ready to use.

3. Spoon 1 pint of the pistachio ice cream into a medium-size bowl and mash with the back of a spoon until it is smooth but not yet melting. Smooth the softened pistachio ice cream over the apricot ice cream with an offset spatula and return the pan to the freezer to firm up, at least 15 minutes.

4. Remove the remaining apricot ice cream from the freezer and mash with the back of a spoon to soften. Spread it over the pistachio ice cream in the pan and freeze until firm, at least 15 minutes.

5. Spoon the remaining pint of pistachio ice cream into a medium-size bowl and mash with the back of a spoon until it is smooth but not yet melting. Smooth it over the apricot ice cream with an offset spatula. Cover the cake with plastic wrap and freeze until very firm, at least 3 hours and up to 1 week.

6. In a large bowl, using an electric mixer, whip the heavy cream, confectioners' sugar, and cardamom until the cream holds soft peaks. Remove the cake from the freezer and release the sides of the pan. Smooth the whipped cream over the top and return the cake to the freezer until the cream is firm, at least 1 hour and up to 6 hours.

mom's peach melba ice cream cake

This recipe comes from Christine Alaimo, former associate publisher of The Harvard Common Press. Her mom used to make it for her when she was a kid, and when I made it myself I could see why it was so memorable.

Serves 10

1½ cups sweetened flaked coconut

¾ cup walnuts, finely chopped

3 tablespoons unsalted butter, melted

2 pints peach ice cream, softened

2 pints vanilla ice cream, softened

One 12-ounce package frozen raspberries in syrup, thawed

½ cup sugar

1 tablespoon cornstarch

2 cups canned sliced peaches, drained and patted dry

1. Preheat the oven to 350°F. Combine the coconut, walnuts, and butter in a medium-size bowl and stir to moisten. Press the mixture evenly into the bottom of a 9-inch springform pan, packing it tightly with your fingertips so it is even and compacted. Bake until crisp, 10 to 12 minutes. Let cool completely. (The crust may be wrapped in plastic wrap and frozen for up to 1 month.)

2. Spoon the peach ice cream into a large mixing bowl and mash with the back of a spoon until it is smooth but not yet melting. Scrape it into the pan and smooth it over the crust with the spoon. Freeze for 10 minutes. Repeat with the vanilla ice cream. Wrap the cake in plastic wrap and freeze until firm, at least 3 hours and up to 1 week.

3. Drain the raspberries, reserving the syrup. Combine the syrup, sugar, and cornstarch in a small saucepan and cook over medium heat, stirring constantly, until thickened, 2 to 3 minutes. Stir in the raspberries. Transfer to a bowl and let cool to room temperature.

4. Just before serving, release the sides of the pan from the cake and arrange the peaches on top of the cake. Serve with the raspberry sauce on the side.

chocolate and cherry ice cream terrine

Serves 6

The whipped cream, cherries, and hot fudge that finish this dessert give it the classic appeal of an ice cream sundae. It's fun and easy to pipe whipped cream rosettes onto the cake for a pastry shop look. For a less formal presentation, simply spoon dollops of cream onto the cake and top each one with a maraschino cherry.

1 pint cherry vanilla ice cream, softened

1 pint chocolate ice cream, softened

12 Nabisco Famous Chocolate Wafers, crushed

½ cup heavy cream, chilled

2 tablespoons confectioners' sugar

½ teaspoon pure vanilla extract

12 maraschino cherries with stems

Hot Fudge Sauce

¼ cup granulated sugar

2 tablespoons unsweetened cocoa powder, Dutch-processed or natural, sifted

¾ cup heavy cream

continued from page 76

½ cup light corn syrup

2 ounces bittersweet chocolate, coarsely chopped

2 tablespoons (¼ stick) unsalted butter

1 teaspoon pure vanilla extract

⅛ teaspoon salt

1. To make the terrine, line a 9½ x 4 x 3-inch loaf pan with a double layer of plastic wrap, making sure the wrap is tucked into all the corners and there is at least 1 inch overhanging the top of the pan on all sides.

2. Spoon the cherry vanilla ice cream into a medium-size mixing bowl and mash with the back of a spoon until it is smooth but not yet melting. Scrape half of it into the pan and smooth the top with the spoon. Freeze for 10 minutes.

3. Spoon the chocolate ice cream into a medium-size mixing bowl and mash with the back of a spoon until it is smooth but not yet melting. Scrape it into the pan and smooth it over the cherry vanilla ice cream with the spoon. Freeze for 10 minutes. Scrape the remaining cherry vanilla ice cream into the pan and smooth it over the chocolate layer with the spoon.

4. Sprinkle the cookie crumbs over the ice cream in an even layer, pressing them lightly into the ice cream. Cover the pan with plastic wrap and freeze until firm, at least 3 hours and up to 1 week.

5. In a large bowl, using an electric mixer, whip the heavy cream with the confectioners' sugar and vanilla extract until it holds stiff peaks.

6. Remove the pan from the freezer and gently tug the plastic wrap that lines the pan to loosen the cake. Place a serving platter over the pan and invert. Gently tap to release the cake. Peel the plastic from the terrine.

7. Use a pastry bag fitted with a large star tip to pipe 12 whipped cream rosettes on top of the terrine. Place a cherry on top of each rosette. (Or simply spoon out 12 dollops of whipped cream and top each dollop with a cherry.) Return the cake to the freezer and freeze until the whipped cream is firm, at least 30 minutes and up to 3 hours.

8. To make the sauce, combine the granulated sugar, cocoa powder, heavy cream, and corn syrup in a heavy medium-size saucepan and whisk to combine. Add the chocolate and bring to a boil over medium-high heat, whisking constantly. Reduce the heat to medium-low and gently boil the sauce, without stirring, for 5 minutes.

9. Remove the pot from the heat and stir in the butter, vanilla extract, and salt. (Hot Fudge Sauce will keep, refrigerated in an airtight container, for up to 2 weeks. Reheat the sauce in a saucepan over medium-low heat, or in a microwave for 1½ minutes, before serving.)

10. Slice the cake and serve with the sauce on the side.

s'mores ice cream terrine

Chocolate, graham crackers, and melting marshmallows give this simple terrine its campfire character. A small kitchen torch quickly browns the marshmallows on top of this cake without melting the ice cream below. If you want to brown the marshmallows under the broiler, be sure to preheat it completely and keep a close eye on the marshmallows so that they brown but don't burn.

Serves 6

2 pints coffee ice cream

1 recipe Hot Fudge Sauce (page 76), cooled to room temperature

4 whole graham crackers

½ cup Marshmallow Fluff

60 miniature marshmallows

continued from page 79

1. Line a 9½ x 4 x 3-inch loaf pan with a double layer of plastic wrap, making sure the wrap is tucked into all the corners and there is at least 1 inch overhanging the top of the pan on all sides.

2. Spoon 1 pint of the ice cream into a medium-size mixing bowl and mash with the back of a spoon until it is smooth and softened but not yet melting. Scrape it into the pan and smooth into an even layer with a small offset spatula. Smooth half of the cooled Hot Fudge Sauce over the ice cream. Place the pan in the freezer until the fudge sauce is firm, about 1 hour.

3. Spoon the remaining pint of ice cream into a medium-size mixing bowl and mash with the back of a spoon until it is smooth but not yet melting. Scrape it into the pan and smooth it over the fudge sauce. Spread the remaining fudge sauce on top of the ice cream.

4. Break the graham crackers into pieces and arrange them over the fudge sauce in an even layer (you may have 1 or 2 small pieces left over). Cover the pan with plastic wrap and freeze until firm, at least 6 hours and up to 1 week.

5. Remove the pan from the freezer and gently tug the plastic wrap that lines the pan to loosen the cake. Place a heatproof serving platter over the pan and invert. Gently tap to release. Peel the plastic from the terrine.

6. Use a small offset spatula to spread the Marshmallow Fluff in an even layer over the top of the terrine. Arrange the miniature marshmallows in rows on top of the Marshmallow Fluff, lightly pressing them into the Fluff. Return to the freezer for up to 2 hours until ready to serve.

7. Use a small crème brûlée torch to brown the marshmallows, moving it over them in a circular motion. Or preheat the broiler to high and place the terrine under the broiler until the marshmallows just start to brown, 30 seconds to 1 minute. Slice and serve immediately.

mango-raspberry terrine with chocolate-coconut sauce

Serves 6

The Chocolate-Coconut Sauce adds richness to this light and refreshing terrine. Just drizzle it on — too much will overwhelm the delicate texture and flavor of the sorbets. Leftover sauce is terrific over vanilla ice cream.

1 cup sweetened flaked coconut

1 pint mango sorbet

1 pint vanilla ice cream

1 pint raspberry sorbet

Chocolate-Coconut Sauce

One 15-ounce can cream of coconut (such as Coco López brand)

6 tablespoons unsweetened cocoa powder, Dutch-processed or natural, sifted

continued from page 81

½ teaspoon pure vanilla extract

½ teaspoon pure coconut extract

Pinch of salt

1. Put the coconut in a small pan and toast over medium heat, stirring often, until golden. Transfer to a bowl and let cool completely.

2. Line a 9½ x 4 x 3-inch loaf pan with a double layer of plastic wrap, making sure the wrap is tucked into all the corners and there is at least 1 inch overhanging the top of the pan on all sides.

3. Spoon the mango sorbet into a medium-size mixing bowl and mash with the back of a spoon until it is smooth but not yet melting. Scrape it into the pan and smooth it into an even layer with an offset spatula. Freeze for 15 minutes.

4. Spoon the vanilla ice cream into a medium-size mixing bowl and mash with the back of a spoon until it is smooth but not yet melting. Scrape it into the pan and smooth it over the mango sorbet with an offset spatula. Freeze for 15 minutes.

5. Spoon the raspberry sorbet into a medium-size mixing bowl and mash with the back of a spoon until it is smooth but not yet melting. Scrape it into the pan and smooth it over the vanilla ice cream with an offset spatula. Sprinkle the toasted coconut over the sorbet in an even layer, pressing it lightly into the sorbet. Cover the pan with plastic wrap and freeze until firm, at least 3 hours and up to 1 week.

6. To make the sauce, combine the cream of coconut and cocoa powder in a medium-size saucepan and heat the mixture over medium-low heat, whisking occasionally, until the cocoa power is dissolved and the sauce is smooth.

7. Remove the pan from the heat and stir in the vanilla extract, coconut extract, and salt. Let cool to lukewarm before serving. (Chocolate-Coconut Sauce will keep in an airtight container at room temperature for up to 3 days. Reheat to lukewarm on the stovetop and whisk before serving.)

8. Remove the pan from the freezer and gently tug the plastic wrap that lines the pan to loosen the cake. Place a serving platter over the pan and invert. Gently tap to release. Peel the plastic from the terrine.

9. Drizzle some of the sauce on each dessert plate. Slice the terrine and place a slice on each plate. Serve immediately.

lemon and blueberry ice cream terrine

Serves 6

It's simple to doctor plain vanilla ice cream, transforming it into layers of fresh-tasting lemon and blueberry ice cream. Crushed creme-filled sugar wafer cookies add crunch. Dollops of softly whipped cream alongside each slice are a simple and pretty finish.

3 pints vanilla ice cream, slightly softened

1 cup fresh blueberries, picked over for stems

¼ cup freshly squeezed lemon juice

1 tablespoon finely grated lemon zest

24 vanilla creme sugar wafers, such as Nabisco Biscos, crushed

¾ cup heavy cream, chilled

1½ tablespoons confectioners' sugar

½ teaspoon pure vanilla extract

1. Line a 9½ x 4 x 3-inch loaf pan with a double layer of plastic wrap, making sure the wrap is tucked into all the corners and there is at least 1 inch overhanging the top of the pan on all sides.

2. Combine 1 pint of ice cream with the blueberries in a food processor and process until smooth. Place in the freezer to keep cold so it doesn't melt while you work.

3. Combine the remaining 2 pints of ice cream, the lemon juice, and the zest in a large bowl and mash with the back of a spoon until it is smooth but not yet melting. Spread half of the lemon ice cream in an even layer across the bottom of the prepared pan. Freeze for 10 minutes. Spread half of the blueberry ice cream mixture on top. Place the pan in the freezer until the blueberry layer is firm, at least 1 hour. Place the remaining blueberry ice cream and the remaining lemon ice cream in the freezer until ready to use.

4. When ready to continue, let the blueberry and lemon ice creams soften for 5 minutes on the counter, then spread the remaining lemon ice cream over the firmed-up blueberry ice cream in the pan. Freeze for 10 minutes. Spread the remaining blueberry ice cream on top of the lemon. Sprinkle the cookie crumbs over the blueberry ice cream in an even layer, pressing them lightly into the ice cream. Cover the pan with plastic wrap and freeze until firm, at least 3 hours and up to 1 week.

5. In a large bowl, using an electric mixer, whip the heavy cream with the confectioners' sugar and vanilla extract until it holds stiff peaks.

6. Remove the pan from the freezer and gently tug the plastic wrap that lines the pan to loosen the cake. Place a serving platter over the pan and invert. Gently tap to release the cake. Slice and serve with whipped cream on the side.

checkerboard ice cream terrine

Serves 8

I borrowed the technique for assembling this cake from a magazine recipe that called for homemade cake and ice cream. But it's a lot easier, and just as visually impressive, to buy the cake and ice cream at the store! To make the terrine slices perfectly rectangular instead of sloping, you'll need an empty 1-quart milk carton instead of a loaf pan. The simple strawberry sauce, brightened up with a little lemon juice and orange zest, makes this a perfect early summer dessert. If you love chocolate with your strawberries, try Warm Chocolate Sauce (page 25) instead.

One 10- to 12-ounce store-bought pound cake, or 1 recipe Homemade Pound Cake (page 15)

2 cups strawberry ice cream, softened

Strawberry Sauce

1 pint fresh strawberries, stemmed and thickly sliced

½ cup sugar

1 teaspoon grated orange zest

1 teaspoon freshly squeezed lemon juice

1. Cut away one long side of an empty 1-quart card-board milk carton. Wash and dry the carton. Slice the cake in half lengthwise. Trim each half so that you have two long strips that measure 1¼ inches in height and width. If they are not as long as the milk carton, cut two more pieces of remaining cake that measure 1¼ inches in height and width and are as long as the difference between the long strips and the carton.

2. Place one of the cake strips (and one of the smaller pieces, if necessary) on the bottom of the carton, so that it is pressing right up against the side of the container. Fill the space next to it with 1 cup of ice cream, smoothing it with an offset spatula, so that it is flush with the cake.

3. Place the second long strip (and the other smaller piece, if necessary) on top of the ice cream. Fill the remaining space on top of the first piece of cake with the remaining 1 cup ice cream, smoothing it with the spatula. Cover the container with plastic wrap and freeze for at least 3 hours and up to 2 days.

4. To make the sauce, combine the strawberries, sugar, orange zest, and lemon juice in a medium-size saucepan over medium heat and cook, stirring frequently, until the sugar dissolves. Bring to a boil. Turn down the heat and cook at a bare simmer for 3 minutes. Transfer to a bowl and refrigerate until chilled, at least 2 hours and up to 1 day.

5. Uncover the cake and carefully peel the container away from it. Slice and serve with the strawberry sauce on the side.

More Fun with Ice Cream

Check out a few more ice cream cake recipes sprinkled throughout this book:

* **Lime-Coconut Terrine with Praline** (page 98)
* **Mini Coffee Cakes** (page 141)
* **Mini Doughnut Ice Cream Sandwiches** (page 143)
* **Banana Ice Cream Cupcakes with Peanut Frosting** (page 139)
* **Brownie Sundae Cupcakes** (page 144)

CHAPTER 4

easy and elegant terrines

Never in a million years did I think, when I bought my 9½ x 4 x 3-inch loaf pan to make a zucchini bread years ago, that it would someday help me create elegant icebox desserts like Chocolate and Chestnut Terrine (page 93). But I now use my loaf pan more often to create refined frozen desserts than I do to bake tea cakes. Make the following recipes—smooth mousses with luxury ingredients—when you want something a little lighter in texture and a little more grown-up than an ice cream cake.

Each one is made with a whipped cream mousse that is scraped into the pan and then frozen for a *semifreddo* effect. The first four are stabilized with a little unflavored gelatin so that when slightly thawed and sliced they won't turn into puddles on the plate. Just remember to handle your gelatin correctly, first softening it in cold water and then heating it through so that it melts completely.

The last three recipes, which use sabayon custard folded into whipped cream, get their body and some extra richness from egg yolks. It's essential that you take your time with sabayon for the smoothest custard, whisking the mixture of egg yolks, sugar, and liquor or liqueur constantly and making sure the bowl doesn't get too hot too fast. Cooling the sabayon over a larger bowl of ice water will let you fold it together with the whipped cream more quickly.

In every recipe, lining the pan with a double layer of plastic wrap will prevent the wrap from tearing and shredding when you unwrap your terrine. Because these desserts are softer than frozen desserts made with ice cream, they can be sliced and served straight from the freezer, but letting them stand for 20 minutes at room temperature before slicing gives the slices pleasantly soft outsides and refreshingly cold interiors.

maple-pumpkin mousse terrine with cranberry–pumpkin seed toffee

Serves 8 to 10

Frozen pumpkin mousse has a great texture, with none of the sogginess or heaviness of refrigerated mousse or pumpkin pie. The quick pumpkin seed candy is great for scooping up bits of mousse.

1 envelope unflavored gelatin

¼ cup cold water

1¼ cups canned pumpkln puree

¾ cup pure maple syrup

½ teaspoon ground cinnamon

½ teaspoon ground ginger

⅛ teaspoon ground cloves

1½ cups heavy cream, chilled

continued from page 90

Cranberry–Pumpkin Seed Toffee

1 cup unsalted hulled pumpkin seeds

1 tablespoon light brown sugar

1 tablespoon unsalted butter, melted

¼ teaspoon salt

1 cup Heath Milk Chocolate English Toffee Bits

½ cup dried cranberries

1. Line a 9½ x 4 x 3-inch loaf pan with a double layer of plastic wrap, making sure the wrap is tucked into all the corners and there is at least 1 inch overhanging the top of the pan on all sides.

2. Sprinkle the gelatin over the water in a small bowl and let soften for 5 minutes.

3. In a medium-size saucepan over medium-low heat, whisk together the pumpkin puree, maple syrup, cinnamon, ginger, and cloves. Cook, whisking constantly, until hot but not quite simmering. Whisk in the gelatin mixture and remove from the heat, whisking occasionally, to cool to room temperature.

4. In a medium-size mixing bowl, using an electric mixer, whip the cream until it just holds soft peaks. Gently fold the whipped cream into the pumpkin mixture.

5. Scrape the mousse into the prepared pan. Cover with plastic and freeze until firm, at least 3 hours and up to 1 day.

6. To make the toffee, line a baking sheet with parchment paper. Combine the pumpkin seeds, brown sugar, butter, and salt in a small saucepan and heat over medium heat until the butter is melted and the sugar is dissolved. Add the toffee bits and cook, stirring, until they are partially melted, 2 to 3 minutes. Stir in the cranberries. Use a metal spatula or the back of a spoon to spread the mixture onto the prepared baking sheet in a thin layer and let stand until hardened, about 15 minutes. Break the candy into 1-inch pieces.

7. Unwrap the terrine. Place a serving platter over the pan and invert. Gently tap to release. Peel the plastic wrap from the terrine. Let the terrine stand until slightly defrosted, about 20 minutes. Slice and serve with the toffee on the side.

chocolate and chestnut terrine

This is a rich, festive dessert that is perfect when you want something sophisticated and unusual for Christmas or New Year's Eve. Marrons glacés are candied chestnuts. They're available at gourmet shops and at many supermarkets during the holidays.

Serves 8 to 10

1½ teaspoons unflavored gelatin

2 tablespoons cold water

½ cup sugar

2½ cups heavy cream, chilled

1 cup sour cream

One 8-ounce (250-gram) can sweetened chestnut spread

1 tablespoon dark rum

½ teaspoon pure vanilla extract

6 ounces bittersweet chocolate, finely chopped

8 *marrons glacés*

continued from page 93

1. Line a 9½ x 4 x 3-inch loaf pan with a double layer of plastic wrap, making sure the wrap is tucked into all the corners and there is at least 1 inch overhanging the top of the pan on all sides.

2. Sprinkle the gelatin over the water in a small bowl and let soften for 5 minutes.

3. Bring 2 inches of water to a simmer in a medium-size saucepan. In a stainless-steel bowl that fits over the top of the saucepan, whisk together the sugar, 2 cups of the heavy cream, and the sour cream. Set the bowl over the pan, making sure the bottom doesn't touch the water. Heat, whisking frequently, until hot. Whisk in the softened gelatin and continue to whisk until completely melted, 30 seconds to 1 minute. Remove the bowl from the heat and whisk in the chestnut spread, rum, and vanilla extract until smooth. Scrape the mixture into the prepared pan, cover with plastic wrap, and freeze until completely set, at least 3 hours and up to 1 day.

4. Put the chocolate in a medium-size heatproof bowl. Bring the remaining ½ cup heavy cream to a boil in a small saucepan and pour over the chocolate. Cover the bowl with plastic wrap and let stand for 5 minutes. Remove the plastic and whisk until smooth.

5. Unwrap the terrine. Place a piece of waxed paper on top of the terrine and invert onto a wire rack. Pour the chocolate glaze over the terrine, smoothing with a small offset spatula so it covers the top and sides completely. The glaze will begin to harden on contact because the terrine is so cold. Dip the bottoms of the candied chestnuts into the leftover glaze at the bottom of the bowl and affix to the top of the terrine randomly. Let the terrine stand until the glaze is firm and the terrine slightly defrosted, about 20 minutes. Use two wide spatulas to transfer the terrine to a serving platter. Serve immediately, or refrigerate for up to 2 hours before serving.

triple chocolate mousse terrine

Serves 8 to 10

Three bands of chocolate are a beautiful and delicious study in contrasts. A couple of tips for making and serving this terrine: Make sure you chop the chocolates very finely, so that they will melt completely when stirred together with the hot custard. Wipe the plastic wrap on the inside of the pan after you smooth each layer of mousse into it, so you get distinct bands of white, light, and dark without streaks. When you slice it, wipe the knife after every slice, so the dark chocolate from the bottom band of one slice doesn't streak the white chocolate of the next slice. I like to serve a little Raspberry Sauce with this. The acidic fruit cuts the sweetness of the chocolate. But if you are a chocolate fanatic, you might want to serve your terrine straight.

4 ounces bittersweet chocolate, finely chopped

4 ounces milk chocolate, finely chopped

4 ounces white chocolate, finely chopped

1 envelope unflavored gelatin

¼ cup cold water

5 large egg yolks

½ cup sugar

1 cup whole milk

1¾ cups heavy cream, chilled

1 recipe Raspberry Sauce (optional; page 35)

continued from page 95

1. Line a 9½ x 4 x 3-inch loaf pan with a double layer of plastic wrap, making sure the wrap is tucked into all the corners and there is at least 1 inch overhanging the top of the pan on all sides.

2. Place the bittersweet, milk, and white chocolates in separate medium-size bowls.

3. Sprinkle the gelatin over the water in a small bowl and let soften for 5 minutes.

4. Combine the egg yolks and sugar in a medium-size bowl. Whisk until pale and slightly increased in volume, 2 to 3 minutes.

5. In a medium-size saucepan, bring the milk to a bare simmer over medium heat. Slowly pour the hot milk into the egg mixture, whisking constantly. Return the milk and egg mixture to the saucepan and cook, whisking constantly, until it just begins to thicken, 1 to 2 minutes. Remove from the heat and whisk in the gelatin mixture. Pour through a fine-mesh strainer into a large measuring cup. You should have about 1½ cups.

6. Pour ½ cup of the hot custard into each of the 3 bowls of chocolate and stir until smooth. Let cool to room temperature, about 10 minutes.

7. In a medium-size bowl, using an electric mixer, whip the heavy cream until it just holds stiff peaks. Fold one-third of the cream into each of the 3 bowls of chocolate.

8. Scrape the white chocolate mousse into the bottom of the prepared loaf pan and smooth into an even layer with a spatula. Freeze until firm, about 15 minutes.

9. Remove the pan from the freezer and scrape the milk chocolate mousse into the pan. Smooth into an even layer with a spatula. Freeze until firm, about 15 minutes.

10. Remove the pan from the freezer and scrape the bittersweet chocolate mousse into the pan. Smooth into an even layer and cover the pan with plastic wrap. Freeze until completely set, at least 6 hours and up to 2 days.

11. Unwrap the terrine. Place a serving platter over the pan and invert. Gently tap to release. Peel the plastic wrap from the terrine. Let stand at room temperature for 20 minutes to soften slightly before slicing and serving with Raspberry Sauce, if desired.

lime-coconut terrine with praline

Serves 8 to 10

Praline made with sesame seeds instead of chopped nuts is flavorful and delicate, and it makes a dramatic garnish for this exotically flavored terrine. The best lime sorbets (I like Ciao Bella and Häagen-Dazs) are often white or very pale green, so I like to add a drop of green food coloring to the sorbet layer to give the finished dessert contrasting colors.

Sesame Seed Praline

¾ cup sugar

¼ cup water

¼ cup sesame seeds

Coconut Mousse

One 15-ounce can cream of coconut (such as Coco López brand)

1 envelope unflavored gelatin

3 tablespoons cold water

1½ cups heavy cream, chilled

¼ teaspoon pure coconut extract

1 pint lime sorbet, softened

Green food coloring (optional)

Fresh blackberries, for garnish

1. To make the praline, butter a heavy, rimmed baking sheet (not nonstick), a spoon, and a small offset spatula. Combine the sugar and water in a small saucepan and stir over medium-low heat until the sugar dissolves. Put the lid on the pot and let cook for 1 minute. Remove the lid, raise the heat to medium-high, and let boil without stirring until the mixture turns a light amber color, 5 to 7 minutes. If parts of the syrup are turning darker than others, gently tilt the pan to even out the cooking.

2. As soon as the syrup is a uniform amber color, remove from the heat and carefully pour in the sesame seeds. When the bubbling subsides, stir once or twice with the buttered spoon to coat the

seeds with the caramel. Pour the mixture onto the prepared baking sheet, using the buttered offset spatula to spread and pull it into as thin a layer as possible. Place the baking sheet on a wire rack and let cool completely.

3. Break the praline into shards. Reserve half of the shards for garnish. Place the remaining praline shards in the work bowl of a food processor fitted with a metal blade and process until finely chopped. (The shards and ground praline may be stored in airtight containers or zipper-lock plastic bags at room temperature for up to 1 week.)

4. Line a 9½ x 4 x 3-inch loaf pan with a double layer of plastic wrap, making sure that the wrap is tucked into all the corners and that there is at least 1 inch overhanging on all sides.

5. To make the mousse, pour the cream of coconut into a small mixing bowl. Sprinkle the gelatin over the water in a small bowl and let soften for 5 minutes. Pour 1 inch of water into a small saucepan and bring to a bare simmer. Place the bowl with the gelatin over the simmering water and heat, whisking constantly, just until the gelatin melts, 30 seconds to 1 minute. Whisk the melted gelatin into the cream of coconut, working quickly so that no rubbery strands form.

6. In a large bowl, using an electric mixer, whip the heavy cream and coconut extract until it holds soft peaks. Thoroughly whisk the coconut mixture into the whipped cream. Pour the mixture into a large measuring cup.

7. To assemble the terrine, pour half of the coconut mousse in an even layer in the bottom of the prepared loaf pan. Place in the freezer and freeze until firm, about 30 minutes. Pour the remaining mousse into a bowl and let stand, whisking several times as it thickens so no large lumps form.

8. Place the softened sorbet in a large bowl and add a drop of green food coloring, if desired. Mash it with the back of a spoon until it is smooth and spreadable. Remove the loaf pan from the freezer and sprinkle half of the crushed praline over the coconut mousse in an even layer. Press lightly on the crushed praline with the back of a spoon so that it adheres to the mousse. Spread the sorbet in an even layer over the praline. Freeze for 10 minutes. Sprinkle the remaining praline over the sorbet. Spread the remaining coconut mousse on top of the crushed praline. Wrap in plastic and freeze until firm, at least 6 hours and up to 2 days.

9. Unwrap the terrine. Place a serving platter over the pan and invert. Gently tap to release. Peel the plastic wrap from the terrine. Arrange the reserved praline shards decoratively on top of the terrine. (I stick the sharp ends into the mousse so the shards stand up at different angles on top of the terrine.) Scatter the blackberries on the platter around the terrine and place a few berries on top, in between the shards. Slice and serve.

frozen armagnac sabayon terrine

Serves 8 to 10

Prunes aren't the most glamorous fruit, but they pack a lot of sweetness and flavor into this semifreddo *spiked with Armagnac, a rather glamorous brandy. You may substitute apricots and regular brandy, if you prefer those flavors, for an equally simple and unusual frozen dessert. Make sure your dried fruit is fresh and moist for the most pleasing texture.*

8 large egg yolks

¾ cup sugar

½ cup Armagnac

2 teaspoons grated orange zest

2½ cups heavy cream, chilled

1 cup prunes, pitted and finely chopped

¼ cup crystallized ginger, finely chopped

1. Line a 9½ x 4 x 3-inch loaf pan with a double layer of plastic wrap, making sure the wrap is tucked into all the corners and there is at least 1 inch overhanging the top of the pan on all sides.

2. In a medium-size saucepan, bring 2 inches of water to a bare simmer. In a stainless-steel bowl big enough to rest on top of the saucepan, whisk together the egg yolks and sugar until foamy. Set the bowl over the pan of water without letting it touch the water. Whisk constantly until it begins to thicken, about 1 minute. Slowly whisk in the Armagnac and continue to cook, whisking constantly, until it registers 160°F on an instant-read thermometer, is pale yellow, and has tripled in volume, 5 to 7 minutes. Whisk in the orange zest. Fill a larger bowl with ice water and place the bowl with the egg mixture on top of the larger bowl. Let cool, whisking occasionally, to room temperature.

3. In a medium-size bowl, using an electric mixer, whip the heavy cream until it just holds stiff peaks (be careful not to overwhip). Gently fold the cream, prunes, and ginger into the cooled sabayon with a rubber spatula, being careful not to deflate the cream.

4. Scrape the mixture into the prepared pan, smooth the top with a spatula, and cover with plastic wrap. Freeze until completely set, at least 6 hours and up to 2 days.

5. Unwrap the terrine. Place a serving platter over the pan and invert. Gently tap to release. Peel the plastic wrap from the terrine. Let stand at room temperature for 20 minutes to soften slightly before slicing and serving.

white wine sabayon terrine with balsamic peaches

Serves 8 to 10

This is one of the simplest recipes in the book, and one of the most elegant. An off-dry white wine with a good amount of fruit works well here with the peaches. Try a Riesling or Gewürztraminer from the Pacific Northwest. These relatively inexpensive wines will give great results. Strawberries are often sprinkled with balsamic vinegar in Italy, but the combination of peaches and vinegar is just as delicious.

8 large egg yolks

¾ cup sugar

1 cup off-dry white wine

1½ cups heavy cream, chilled

Balsamic Peaches

4 ripe peaches (about 1¼ pounds)

2 tablespoons sugar

2 teaspoons balsamic vinegar

continued from page 102

1. Line a 9½ x 4 x 3-inch loaf pan with a double layer of plastic wrap, making sure the wrap is tucked into all the corners and there is at least 1 inch overhanging the top of the pan on all sides.

2. In a medium-size saucepan, bring 2 inches of water to a bare simmer. In a stainless-steel bowl big enough to rest on top of the saucepan, whisk together the egg yolks and sugar until foamy. Set the bowl over the pan of water without letting it touch the water. Whisk constantly until it begins to thicken, about 1 minute. Slowly whisk in the wine and continue to cook, whisking constantly, until it registers 160°F on an instant-read thermometer, is pale yellow, and has tripled in volume, 5 to 7 minutes. Fill a larger bowl with ice water and place the bowl with the egg mixture on top of the larger bowl. Let cool, whisking occasionally, to room temperature.

3. In a medium-size bowl, using an electric mixer, whip the heavy cream until it just holds stiff peaks (be careful not to overwhip). Gently fold the cream into the cooled sabayon with a rubber spatula, being careful not to deflate the cream.

4. Scrape the mixture into the prepared pan, smooth the top with a spatula, and cover with plastic wrap. Freeze until completely set, at least 6 hours and up to 2 days.

5. To make the peaches, just before serving, peel, halve, and pit the peaches. Cut the halves into ¼-inch-thick wedges. Place in a nonreactive bowl and stir in the sugar and vinegar. Let stand, stirring occasionally, to dissolve the sugar.

6. Unwrap the terrine. Place a serving platter over the pan and invert. Gently tap to release. Peel the plastic wrap from the terrine. Let stand at room temperature for 20 minutes to soften slightly. Slice and serve, spooning some of the peaches over each slice.

rum-pineapple terrine with tropical fruit salad

Serves 8 to 10

Although it may sound a bit over the top, somehow the piled-on tropical flavors of the fruit, lime juice, ginger, and rum are not too much in this happy frozen dessert.

8 large egg yolks

½ cup plus 2 tablespoons sugar

½ cup light rum

1¾ cups heavy cream, chilled

One 20-ounce can crushed pineapple, drained

Tropical Fruit Salad

2 tablespoons water

2 tablespoons sugar

1 tablespoon freshly squeezed lime juice

1 teaspoon grated fresh ginger

continued from page 105

1 large mango, peeled, pitted, and cut into ¼-inch dice

2 kiwis, peeled and thinly sliced

1. Line a 9½ x 4 x 3-inch loaf pan with a double layer of plastic wrap, making sure the wrap is tucked into all the corners and there is at least 1 inch overhanging the top of the pan on all sides.

2. In a medium-size saucepan, bring 2 inches of water to a bare simmer. In a stainless-steel bowl big enough to rest on top of the saucepan, whisk together the egg yolks and sugar until foamy. Set the bowl over the pan of water without letting it touch the water. Whisk constantly until it begins to thicken, about 1 minute. Slowly whisk in the rum and continue to cook, whisking constantly, until it registers 160°F on an instant-read thermometer, is pale yellow, and has tripled in volume, 5 to 7 minutes. Fill a larger bowl with ice water and place the bowl with the egg mixture on top of the larger bowl. Let cool, whisking occasionally, to room temperature.

3. In a medium-size bowl, using an electric mixer, whip the heavy cream until it just holds stiff peaks (be careful not to overwhip). Gently fold the cream and pineapple into the cooled sabayon with a rubber spatula, being careful not to deflate the cream.

4. Scrape the mixture into the prepared pan, smooth the top with a spatula, and cover with plastic wrap. Freeze until completely set, at least 6 hours and up to 2 days.

5. To make the fruit salad, just before serving, combine the water and sugar in a small saucepan and bring to a boil, stirring, to dissolve the sugar. Remove from the heat and stir in the lime juice and ginger. Pour into a small bowl and let cool to room temperature. Place the mango and kiwis in a medium-size bowl and toss with the lime dressing.

6. Unwrap the terrine. Place a serving platter over the pan and invert. Gently tap to release. Peel the plastic wrap from the terrine. Let stand at room temperature for 20 minutes to soften slightly. Slice and serve with the fruit salad on the side.

CHAPTER 5

no-bake, no-fail cheesecakes

Bake until the cake is just set around the edges but a little wobbly in the center." When I am reading through a cheesecake recipe, this line always strikes fear in my heart. So do the phrases "water bath" and "Do not overbake." If I work up the courage to proceed, I find myself questioning my judgment of the cake as it bakes. Inevitably, the cake looks way too wiggly when I first jiggle it. In fact, it looks raw. But when I check on it 3 minutes later, it looks overbaked! While I'm checking, I never fail to splash hot water from the water bath over the top of the cake, ruining its looks. As it cools, I fret about its texture. When I slice into it, will it be silky smooth or a curdled mess? This is the agony of baking a cheesecake.

Thankfully, there's an easier way. Simply mix together a luscious filling without eggs and there's no need to bake your cheesecake at all. Just refrigerate it until it is firm, slice, and serve. The cheesecakes in this chapter rely on the refrigerator instead of the oven to thicken their fillings. By varying your flavoring ingredients, you can make cakes to suit every taste. In each case, the end result is a creamy and absolutely delicious cake without any stress or suspense.

The general procedure is simple. Here are a few tips to smooth your path:

Make a perfect cookie crumb crust. I like to tailor the crust to the filling. Nutter Butter cookies add a little something extra to a chocolate–peanut butter cake. Gingersnaps are a spicy counterpoint to a blackberry and lemon filling. Graham crackers are classic with vanilla. (If you disagree, you may mix and match the crusts and fillings in these recipes as you like.) After finely grinding your cookies in a food processor and mixing them with melted butter and any other crust ingredients, be sure to pat them firmly into the bottom and up the sides of a springform pan so that there are no loose crumbs. Bake the crust just enough so that it won't fall apart, but not so much that it is too hard to cut. Six to 8 minutes should do the trick.

Then let the crust cool completely before you fill it with the cheese mixture. A crust filled while it is still warm will become soggy. In addition, it may deflate the whipped cream in your cake or compromise the cream cheese.

Bring your cream cheese to room temperature. The only way you are going to get lumps in a no-bake cheesecake is if you attempt to make the filling without letting the cream cheese soften. Let it come to room temperature on the kitchen counter. This should take 30 minutes to 1 hour.

If you are in a rush, cut the cream cheese into 1-inch pieces to soften it more quickly.

Handle your gelatin properly. Most no-bake cheesecakes contain a little unflavored gelatin to give them body. As long as you follow a simple two-step process to prepare it, gelatin is a foolproof and flavorless thickener. First, soak it in cold water to soften it up. Then, heat it either on top of a double boiler or by stirring it into other heated ingredients to dissolve it completely. When heating gelatin, whisk it vigorously for about 1 minute to make sure that no globs or rubbery strands remain.

Just chill. Give your cake enough time to cool down. Refrigerating your cake adequately will not only firm up the filling, but it will also allow time for the melding and intensification of the filling flavors.

Praline Variations

Praline garnishes can provide a dramatic touch and a deliciously flavorful crunch to numerous icebox desserts. Here are some ideas.

* **Sliced Almond Praline or Pumpkin Seed Praline:** Substitute an equal amount of blanched sliced almonds or unsalted hulled pumpkin seeds for the sesame seeds and proceed as directed for Sesame Seed Praline on page 98. Break up Sliced Almond Praline and use as a garnish for Lemon and Blueberry Ice Cream Terrine (page 84), and/or grind some of the praline and sprinkle it between the layers of ice cream. Break up Pumpkin Seed Praline and use as a garnish for Maple-Pumpkin Mousse Terrine (page 90), instead of using the Cranberry–Pumpkin Seed Toffee.

* **Pecan Praline, Walnut Praline, or Hazelnut Praline:** Follow the directions on page 98 for making Sesame Seed Praline, using 1 cup sugar, ¼ cup water, and 1½ cups chopped pecans or walnuts or 1½ cups skinned and chopped hazelnuts. The mixture will be thicker when spread onto the buttered baking sheet. Grind Pecan Praline and press into the sides of Orange Bavarian Cake with Chocolate Polka Dots (page 53) just before serving. Break up Walnut Praline and use as a garnish for Maple Syrup Cheesecake (page 125) and/or grind some of the praline and sprinkle it on top of the cake just before serving. Break up Hazelnut Praline and use as a garnish for Triple Chocolate Mousse Terrine (page 95), and/or grind some of the praline and sprinkle it between the layers of mousse.

lemon-blackberry cheesecake

When local blackberries are in season, I snap them up to make this simple no-bake cheesecake. Its eye-popping purple hue is a reminder that nature can produce colors brighter and more beautiful than any food dye. The sweetness of berries will vary, so taste and adjust the sugar in the filling as necessary.

Serves 10

Gingersnap Crust

25 gingersnap cookies (to yield about 1⅓ cups crumbs)

5 tablespoons unsalted butter, melted

¼ teaspoon ground cinnamon

1 teaspoon pure vanilla extract

⅛ teaspoon salt

1 envelope unflavored gelatin

¼ cup cold water

12 ounces cream cheese, softened

1 cup heavy cream, chilled

3 cups fresh blackberries, plus more for garnish

continued from page 111

⅔ cup sugar, or more to taste

1 tablespoon strained freshly squeezed lemon juice

½ teaspoon grated lemon zest

1. To make the crust, preheat the oven to 350°F. Place the gingersnaps in the work bowl of a food processor and process until finely ground. Combine the crumbs, butter, cinnamon, vanilla extract, and salt in a medium-size mixing bowl and stir until moistened.

2. Press the mixture evenly across the bottom and about 1 inch up the sides of a 9-inch springform pan, packing it tightly with your fingertips so it is even and compacted. Bake until crisp, 6 to 8 minutes. Let cool completely. (The crust may be wrapped in plastic wrap and frozen for up to 1 month.)

3. Sprinkle the gelatin over cold water in a small heatproof bowl and let soften for 5 minutes. In the work bowl of a food processor, combine the cream cheese, heavy cream, blackberries, sugar, lemon juice, and lemon zest and process the mixture until it is smooth.

4. Put 1 inch of water in a small saucepan and bring to a bare simmer. Place the bowl containing the gelatin on top of the simmering water and heat, whisking constantly, just until the gelatin melts, 30 seconds to 1 minute. With the food processor running, pour the gelatin mixture through the feed tube into the blackberry mixture and process to create a smooth puree. Taste the filling and add more sugar to your taste.

5. Scrape the filling into the prepared crust. Cover with plastic wrap and refrigerate until the filling is completely set, at least 6 hours and up to 1 day.

6. Release the sides of the pan, slice the cheesecake, and serve with a scattering of whole blackberries on each plate.

vanilla bean cheesecake with plum compote

This is a mild and light cheesecake, with a beautiful perfume from vanilla bean seeds. A simple topping of plums in syrup, also flavored with the vanilla bean, is a colorful accompaniment. Use any leftover plums as an ice cream topping or stirred into oatmeal for breakfast the next day.

Graham Cracker Crust

11 whole graham crackers (to yield about 1⅓ cups crumbs)

5 tablespoons unsalted butter, melted

2 tablespoons light brown sugar

⅛ teaspoon salt

Serves 10

Vanilla Bean Filling

2½ cups heavy cream, chilled

1 envelope unflavored gelatin

½ vanilla bean, split in half lengthwise

8 ounces cream cheese, softened and cut into 6 pieces

½ cup sour cream

6 tablespoons granulated sugar

Plum Compote

4 cups water

1½ cups granulated sugar

2 pounds plums, halved, pitted, and cut into ½-inch wedges

continued from page 114

1. To make the crust, preheat the oven to 350°F. Place the graham crackers in the work bowl of a food processor and process until finely ground. Combine the crumbs, butter, brown sugar, and salt in a medium-size mixing bowl and stir until moistened.

2. Press the mixture evenly across the bottom and about 1 inch up the sides of a 9-inch springform pan, packing it tightly with your fingertips so it is even and compacted. Bake until crisp, 6 to 8 minutes. Let cool completely. (The crust may be wrapped in plastic wrap and frozen for up to 1 month.)

3. To make the filling, place ½ cup of the heavy cream in a small bowl, sprinkle the gelatin on top, and let soften for 5 minutes.

4. Place 1 cup of the heavy cream in a small saucepan. Scrape the seeds of the vanilla bean into the pan and then put the scraped bean in the pan. Heat until the cream comes to a bare simmer. Remove from the heat and let stand for 5 minutes. Remove the vanilla bean, rinse, and set aside. Whisk the hot cream into the gelatin mixture and continue to whisk until the gelatin is dissolved, about 1 minute.

5. Place the cream cheese in a mixing bowl and beat with an electric mixer until smooth. With the mixer on low, slowly stir in the gelatin mixture. Increase the speed to medium-high and mix until smooth, cool, and thickened, 1 to 2 minutes.

6. Combine the remaining 1 cup heavy cream, the sour cream, and the granulated sugar in a large mixing bowl. Use an electric mixer to whip until soft peaks form. Gently fold in the cream cheese mixture. Scrape the filling into the prepared crust. Cover with plastic wrap and refrigerate until the filling is completely set, at least 6 hours and up to 1 day.

7. To make the compote, combine the water and granulated sugar in a medium-size saucepan. Add the reserved scraped vanilla bean. Bring to a simmer over medium heat and cook, stirring, until the sugar has dissolved. Add the plums and simmer until the plums are just tender, 1 to 2 minutes. Use a slotted spoon to transfer the plums to a large bowl. Turn the heat to high and boil the syrup until it is reduced to about 2 cups, 5 to 7 minutes. Cool the syrup to room temperature, remove the vanilla bean, and pour over the plums. (The plums and syrup may be refrigerated in an airtight container for up to 1 day.)

8. Release the sides of the pan from the cake and cut the cheesecake into wedges. Spoon some compote over each slice just before serving.

Vanilla Beans

If you have ever baked cookies or a cake, then you are familiar with the pleasant and homey aroma of vanilla extract, which is made by soaking crushed vanilla beans in alcohol for several months. Vanilla beans themselves have an undiluted aroma that is not so much pleasant and homey as it is intoxicating and exotic. If you want to experience the undiluted essence of vanilla, beans are the way to go.

Vanilla beans are a particularly effective flavoring ingredient in icebox cake fillings that are heated before they are chilled. In contrast to pure vanilla extract, which needs to be stirred in off the heat so that the alcohol (and most of the vanilla flavor) won't evaporate, vanilla beans and seeds give off flavor as they are heated and continue to infuse fillings with flavor as the fillings cool.

Look for plump, moist, sticky beans. Beans that are brittle and dried out will have lost most of their flavor. For this reason, I avoid buying vanilla beans at the supermarket—you never know how long they've been sitting in their jars in the spice aisle. A better bet is to mail-order them or buy them at a specialty store like Williams-Sonoma, where the inventory is carefully monitored.

To split a vanilla bean, place it on a cutting board and run the dull edge of a paring knife down the bean to flatten it against the board. Then split the flattened bean by cutting through the bean from top to bottom as it lies flat on the cutting board, so you wind up with two flat strips. Scrape the seeds from the inside with the sharp edge of the paring knife and add them to your filling. If you are not going to add the bean as well, wrap it in plastic and save it. You can use it to infuse another filling with vanilla flavor at a later date.

You can substitute the scraped seeds of half a vanilla bean for the pure vanilla extract in the following recipes. Where noted, you can also use the scraped bean to intensify the vanilla flavor of the finished dessert.

✳ **Strawberry-Custard Doughnut Cake** (page 58): Scrape the seeds from half a split vanilla bean and also add the scraped bean into the half-and-half when making the pastry cream. Remove the bean before straining the thickened pastry cream.

✳ **Rice Pudding Mousse Cake with Rum-Raisin Sauce** (page 44): Scrape the seeds from half a split vanilla bean and also add the scraped bean into the pot with the parboiled rice, milk, cinnamon stick, and sugar. Remove the bean after cooking.

✳ **Strawberry Coeurs à la Crème with Warm Chocolate Sauce** (page 154): Substitute the seeds from half a split vanilla bean for the pure vanilla extract and proceed as directed.

chocolate–peanut butter cheesecake

Here's a rich dessert for fans of Reese's Peanut Butter Cups. A peanut butter cookie crust is a fun alternative to the usual graham cracker crust. Chopped salted peanuts pressed into the sides of the cake are a pretty garnish and provide a nice contrast to the sweetness of the chocolate. No gelatin is necessary, because so much body is provided by the chocolate, cream cheese, and peanut butter.

Serves 10

Nutter Butter Crust

16 Nutter Butter cookies (to yield about 1¼ cups crumbs)

3 tablespoons unsalted butter, melted

12 ounces bittersweet chocolate, finely chopped

1½ cups heavy cream, chilled

16 ounces cream cheese, softened

½ cup creamy peanut butter

5 tablespoons sugar

½ cup salted dry-roasted peanuts, finely chopped

1. To make the crust, preheat the oven to 350°F. Place the cookies in the work bowl of a food processor and process until finely ground. Combine the crumbs and butter in a medium-size mixing bowl and stir until moistened.

2. Press the mixture evenly across the bottom and about 1 inch up the sides of a 9-inch springform pan, packing it tightly with your fingertips so it is even and compacted. Bake until crisp, 6 to 8 minutes. Let cool completely. (The crust may be wrapped in plastic wrap and frozen for up to 1 month.)

3. Put 2 inches of water in a medium-size saucepan and bring to a bare simmer. Combine the chocolate and ½ cup of the heavy cream in a stainless-steel bowl big enough to rest on top of the saucepan. Place the bowl over the simmering water, making sure that the bottom of the bowl doesn't touch the water. Heat, whisking occasionally, until the chocolate is completely melted. Remove the bowl from the heat and let cool slightly.

4. Using an electric mixer, beat the softened cream cheese and peanut butter into the chocolate mixture until smooth.

5. In a large bowl, using an electric mixer, whip the remaining 1 cup heavy cream with the sugar until it holds soft peaks. Gently fold the whipped cream into the chocolate–peanut butter mixture.

6. Scrape the filling into the prepared crust, smoothing the top with a rubber spatula. Cover with plastic wrap and refrigerate until firm, at least 6 hours and up to 1 day.

7. Release the sides of the pan from the cheesecake. Press the chopped peanuts into the sides of the cake, slice, and serve.

peach and almond cheesecake

This is a perfect late summer dessert, when fresh peaches are at their peak and you want something cool and creamy to finish a meal. Arrange the peaches on top of the cake no more than an hour before serving, or else the moisture from the fruit will make the top of the cake soggy.

Serves 10

Graham-Amaretti Crust

4 whole graham crackers (to yield about ½ cup crumbs)

24 amaretti cookies (to yield about 1 cup crumbs)

5 tablespoons unsalted butter, melted

½ teaspoon pure almond extract

Pinch of salt

1½ cups heavy cream, chilled

1 envelope unflavored gelatin

⅔ cup sugar

16 ounces cream cheese, softened and cut into 1-inch chunks

1 teaspoon pure almond extract

1 teaspoon pure vanilla extract

2 or 3 fresh peaches

¼ cup apricot preserves

1 tablespoon amaretto or other almond-flavored liqueur

½ cup sliced almonds

1. To make the crust, preheat the oven to 350°F. Place the graham crackers and amaretti cookies in the work bowl of a food processor and process until finely ground. Combine the crumbs, butter, almond extract, and salt in a medium-size mixing bowl and stir until moistened.

2. Press the mixture evenly across the bottom and about 1 inch up the sides of a 9-inch springform pan, packing it tightly with your fingertips so it is even and compacted. Bake until crisp, 6 to 8 minutes. Let cool completely. (The crust may be wrapped in plastic wrap and frozen for up to 1 month.)

3. Place ¼ cup of the heavy cream in a small heatproof bowl, sprinkle the gelatin on top, and let soften for 5 minutes. Put 1 inch of water in a small saucepan and bring to a bare simmer. Place the bowl over the simmering water and heat, whisking constantly, just until the gelatin melts, 30 seconds to 1 minute.

4. Combine the remaining 1¼ cups heavy cream and the sugar in a large mixing bowl and, using an electric mixer, beat until soft peaks form. Beat in the cream cheese until the mixture is almost smooth (a few small lumps are okay), 1 minute more. Stir in the almond extract and vanilla extract. With the mixer running, pour in the liquefied gelatin. Continue to beat until the mixture is light and smooth, 2 to 3 minutes.

5. Scrape the filling into the prepared crust, smoothing the top with a rubber spatula. Cover with plastic wrap and refrigerate until firm, at least 6 hours and up to 2 days.

6. Slice the peaches thinly. Arrange the slices in concentric circles on top of the cake. Heat the preserves and amaretto in a small pan until loose and just warm. Push the mixture through a fine-mesh strainer into a small bowl. Brush over the peaches. Return the cake to the refrigerator and chill for 30 minutes to 1 hour.

7. Release the sides of the pan from the cheesecake. Press the almonds into the sides of the cake, slice, and serve.

cappuccino crunch cheesecake

This cheesecake was inspired by a favorite ice cream flavor. Don't skip the Mocha Sauce—it balances the slightly bitter edge of the espresso in the cheesecake.

Serves 10

Chocolate Cookie Crust

30 Nabisco Famous Chocolate Wafers (to yield about 1⅓ cups crumbs)

5 tablespoons unsalted butter, melted

Pinch of salt

Espresso Filling

1½ cups heavy cream

2 tablespoons instant espresso powder

1 envelope unflavored gelatin

⅔ cup sugar

16 ounces cream cheese, softened and cut into 1-inch chunks

1 teaspoon pure vanilla extract

continued from page 122

Four 1.4-ounce Heath Bars, finely chopped, or 1 cup Heath Milk Chocolate English Toffee Bits

Mocha Sauce

8 ounces bittersweet chocolate, finely chopped

¼ cup water

1 tablespoon Kahlúa or other coffee-flavored liqueur

1. To make the crust, preheat the oven to 350°F. Place the chocolate cookies in the work bowl of a food processor and process until finely ground. Combine the crumbs, butter, and salt in a medium-size mixing bowl and stir until moistened.

2. Press the mixture evenly across the bottom and about 1 inch up the sides of a 9-inch springform pan, packing it tightly with your fingertips so it is even and compacted. Bake until crisp, 6 to 8 minutes. Let cool completely. (The crust may be wrapped in plastic wrap and frozen for up to 1 month.)

3. To make the filling, place ½ cup of the heavy cream in a small heatproof bowl and whisk in the espresso powder to dissolve. Sprinkle the gelatin on top and let soften for 5 minutes. Put 1 inch of water in a small saucepan and bring to a bare simmer. Place the bowl over the simmering water and heat, whisking constantly, just until the gelatin melts, 30 seconds to 1 minute.

4. Combine the remaining 1 cup heavy cream and the sugar in a large mixing bowl and, using an electric mixer, beat until soft peaks form. Beat in the cream cheese until the mixture is almost smooth (a few small lumps are okay), 1 minute more. Stir in the vanilla extract. With the mixer running, pour in the liquefied gelatin. Continue to beat until the mixture is light and smooth, 2 to 3 minutes. Fold in the chopped Heath Bars.

5. Scrape the filling into the prepared crust, smoothing the top with a rubber spatula. Cover with plastic wrap and refrigerate until firm, at least 6 hours and up to 2 days.

6. To make the sauce, put 2 inches of water in a medium-size saucepan and bring to a bare simmer. Combine the chocolate and water in a stainless-steel bowl big enough to rest on top of the saucepan and place over the simmering water, making sure the water doesn't touch the bottom of the bowl. Heat the chocolate, whisking occasionally, until it is completely melted. Turn off the heat and stir in the Kahlúa. (You may refrigerate the sauce in an airtight container for up to 2 days. Reheat in a microwave or over a pot of simmering water before serving.)

7. Release the sides of the pan from the cheesecake. Slice and serve with the sauce on the side.

maple syrup cheesecake

Reducing the maple syrup concentrates the flavor and makes this cheesecake unbelievably maple-y. That doesn't stop me from drizzling slices with some more maple syrup for a simple, pretty finish.

Serves 10

Graham-Walnut Crust

11 whole graham crackers (to yield about 1⅓ cups crumbs)

⅓ cup walnut pieces

5 tablespoons unsalted butter, melted

1 tablespoon light brown sugar

½ teaspoon pure maple extract (optional)

⅛ teaspoon salt

1½ cups pure maple syrup, plus more, warmed, for drizzling

1½ cups heavy cream, chilled

1 envelope unflavored gelatin

continued from page 125

16 ounces cream cheese, softened and cut into 1-inch chunks

½ teaspoon pure maple extract

1. To make the crust, preheat the oven to 350°F. Place the graham crackers and walnuts in the work bowl of a food processor and process until finely ground. Combine the crumb mixture, butter, brown sugar, maple extract, if you are using it, and salt in a medium-size mixing bowl and stir until moistened.

2. Press the mixture evenly across the bottom and about 1 inch up the sides of a 9-inch springform pan, packing it tightly with your fingertips so it is even and compacted. Bake until crisp, 6 to 8 minutes. Let cool completely. (The crust may be wrapped in plastic wrap and frozen for up to 1 month.)

3. Pour 1½ cups of the maple syrup into a medium-size saucepan and bring to a boil. Reduce the heat to medium and continue to cook until it is reduced to ¾ cup, 6 to 8 minutes. Carefully stir in ¼ cup of the heavy cream (it will bubble up, so use a long-handled spoon) and continue to cook, stirring, until the mixture is smooth. Remove from the heat and transfer to a heatproof measuring cup. Let cool completely.

4. Place ¼ cup of the heavy cream in a small heatproof bowl, sprinkle the gelatin on top, and let soften for 5 minutes. Put 1 inch of water in a small saucepan and bring to a bare simmer. Place the bowl over the simmering water and heat, whisking constantly, just until the gelatin melts, 30 seconds to 1 minute.

5. Combine the remaining 1 cup heavy cream and the cooled maple syrup mixture in a large mixing bowl and, using an electric mixer, beat until the mixture is thick. Beat in the cream cheese until the mixture is almost smooth (a few small lumps are okay), 1 minute more. Stir in the maple extract. With the mixer running, pour in the liquefied gelatin. Continue to beat until the mixture is light and smooth, 2 to 3 minutes.

6. Scrape the filling into the prepared crust, smoothing the top with a rubber spatula. Cover with plastic wrap and refrigerate until firm, at least 6 hours and up to 2 days.

7. Release the sides of the pan from the cheesecake. Slice and serve drizzled with warm maple syrup.

coconut cheesecake with mango sauce

Here is a wonderful summer cheesecake, great after a Latin-themed barbecue. The bright and acidic Mango Sauce cuts the sweetness of the coconut and gives the cake some extra tropical flair. Be sure to stir up the cream of coconut before measuring it out, because it settles and separates in the can.

Serves 10

Graham-Coconut Crust

11 whole graham crackers (to yield about 1⅓ cups crumbs)

¼ cup (½ stick) unsalted butter, melted

⅓ cup sweetened flaked coconut

1 teaspoon pure coconut extract

⅛ teaspoon salt

Coconut Filling

1 cup cream of coconut (such as Coco López brand)

1 envelope unflavored gelatin

½ cup heavy cream, chilled

16 ounces cream cheese, softened and cut into 1-inch chunks

continued from page 127

1 teaspoon pure coconut extract

1 teaspoon pure vanilla extract

Mango Sauce

One 14-ounce bag frozen mango puree, thawed

2 tablespoons confectioners' sugar

1 tablespoon dark rum

1. To make the crust, preheat the oven to 350°F. Place the graham crackers in the work bowl of a food processor and process until finely ground. Combine the crumbs, butter, coconut, coconut extract, and salt in a medium-size mixing bowl and stir until moistened.

2. Press the mixture evenly across the bottom and about 1 inch up the sides of a 9-inch springform pan, packing it tightly with your fingertips so it is even and compacted. Bake until crisp, 6 to 8 minutes. Let cool completely. (The crust may be wrapped in plastic wrap and frozen for up to 1 month.)

3. To make the filling, place ½ cup of the cream of coconut in a small heatproof bowl, sprinkle the gelatin on top, and let soften for 5 minutes. Put 1 inch of water in a small saucepan and bring to a bare simmer. Place the bowl over the simmering water and heat, whisking constantly, just until the gelatin melts, 30 seconds to 1 minute.

4. In a large bowl, using an electric mixer, beat the heavy cream until soft peaks form. Beat in the cream cheese and the remaining ½ cup cream of coconut until the mixture is almost smooth (a few small lumps are okay), 1 minute more. Stir in the coconut extract and vanilla extract. With the mixer running, pour in the liquefied gelatin. Continue to beat until the mixture is light and smooth, 2 to 3 minutes.

5. Scrape the filling into the prepared crust, smoothing the top with a rubber spatula. Cover with plastic wrap and refrigerate until firm, at least 6 hours and up to 2 days.

6. To make the sauce, push the mango puree through a fine-mesh strainer to remove any strings or tough fibers. Stir in the confectioners' sugar and rum. (You may refrigerate the sauce in an airtight container for up to 3 days.)

7. Release the sides of the pan from the cheesecake. Drizzle the sauce on dessert plates and then place a slice of cake over the sauce on each plate. Serve immediately.

black and white cheesecake

A layer of vanilla topped by a layer of chocolate makes a simple but beautiful cake for fans of both flavors. If you need a little color with your cake, serve it with some sliced, lightly sugared strawberries on the side.

Serves 10

Graham Cracker Crust

11 whole graham crackers (to yield about 1⅓ cups crumbs)

5 tablespoons unsalted butter, melted

2 tablespoons light brown sugar

⅛ teaspoon salt

6 ounces bittersweet chocolate, finely chopped

1½ cups heavy cream, chilled

1 envelope unflavored gelatin

⅔ cup granulated sugar

16 ounces cream cheese, softened and cut into 1-inch chunks

1 teaspoon pure vanilla extract

1. To make the crust, preheat the oven to 350°F. Place the graham crackers in the work bowl of a food processor and process until finely ground. Combine the crumbs, butter, brown sugar, and salt in a medium-size mixing bowl and stir until moistened.

2. Press the mixture evenly across the bottom and about 1 inch up the sides of a 9-inch springform pan, packing it tightly with your fingertips so it is even and compacted. Bake until crisp, 6 to 8 minutes. Let cool completely. (The crust may be wrapped in plastic wrap and frozen for up to 1 month.)

3. Put 2 inches of water in a medium-size saucepan and bring to a bare simmer. Combine the chocolate and ¼ cup of the heavy cream in a stainless-steel bowl big enough to rest on top of the saucepan. Place the bowl over the simmering water, making sure the bottom of the bowl doesn't touch the water. Heat, whisking occasionally, until the chocolate is completely melted. Remove the bowl from the heat and let cool slightly.

4. Place ¼ cup of the heavy cream in a small heatproof bowl, sprinkle the gelatin on top, and let soften for 5 minutes. Put 1 inch of water in a small saucepan and bring to a bare simmer. Place the bowl over the simmering water and heat, whisking constantly, just until the gelatin melts, 30 seconds to 1 minute.

5. Combine the remaining 1 cup heavy cream and the granulated sugar in a large mixing bowl and, using an electric mixer, beat until soft peaks form. Beat in the cream cheese until the mixture is almost smooth (a few small lumps are okay), 1 minute more. Stir in the vanilla extract. With the mixer running, pour in the liquefied gelatin. Continue to beat until the mixture is light and smooth, 2 to 3 minutes.

6. Transfer one-third of the mixture to a medium-size bowl and whisk in the cooled chocolate mixture.

7. Scrape the vanilla filling into the prepared crust, smoothing the top with a rubber spatula. Spoon heaping tablespoonfuls of the chocolate mixture evenly over the vanilla mixture, smoothing it into an even layer with a rubber spatula. Cover with plastic wrap and refrigerate until firm, at least 6 hours and up to 2 days.

8. Remove the sides of the pan from the cheesecake, slice, and serve.

CHAPTER 6

icebox miniatures

cupcakes and other little desserts

As I was working on my icebox cake recipes, I often noticed pictures of cupcakes on the covers of food magazines and quite a few new baking books. There's no denying their visual and nostalgic appeal. Cupcakes are undoubtedly cute, and they remind us of the fun we had eating them when we were kids.

So I had a lot of fun with the idea of shrinking the icebox cake down to cupcake size. I use many of the same ingredients as in the larger desserts—cookies, pound cake, pudding, whipped cream—making pretty little single-serving cakes perfect for all kinds of entertaining, from a kid's birthday party to a romantic Valentine's Day dinner.

Not all of these recipes are cupcakes in the strict sense, made in muffin tins and encased in paper liners. But I guarantee that these small treats, which range from tiny ice cream sandwiches made with mini doughnuts to petit fours and Napoleons, will make your guests feel special while relieving you of the hassle of slicing and plating a larger cake.

your basic
ice cream cupcakes

Here's a method for making quick ice cream desserts cleverly disguised as conventional-looking cupcakes. If your children have summer birthdays, you should try these. You may never bake a birthday cake again. Chocolate and vanilla are birthday-party standbys, but other ice cream flavors may be substituted as desired.

Makes 12 cupcakes

One 10- to 12-ounce store-bought pound cake, or 1 recipe Homemade Pound Cake (page 15)

¼ cup strawberry, raspberry, or apricot jam

2 pints vanilla or chocolate ice cream

1½ cups heavy cream, chilled

⅓ cup confectioners' sugar

½ teaspoon pure vanilla extract

2 tablespoons rainbow sprinkles

Chopped toasted almonds for garnish (optional)

1. Arrange 12 paper liners in a 12-cup muffin tin. Cut the pound cake into ½-inch-thick slices. Use a 2-inch biscuit cutter to cut 12 circles from the slices. Reserve the remaining pound cake and scraps for another use.

2. Spread 1 teaspoon of jam on top of each pound cake circle. Place a circle in the bottom of each cupcake liner. Place a nicely rounded ⅓-cup scoop of ice cream on top of each pound cake circle. Cover the muffin tin with plastic wrap and place in the freezer until the ice cream is very firm, at least 2 hours and up to 2 days.

3. Combine the heavy cream, confectioners' sugar, and vanilla extract in a medium-size bowl and, using an electric mixer, whip until it holds stiff peaks.

4. Remove the muffin tin from the freezer and cover the ice cream with the whipped cream (leaving the cakes in the tin). Scatter the sprinkles over the whipped cream. Cover with plastic wrap and return to the freezer to allow the topping to set, at least 2 hours and up to 1 day.

5. Lift the cupcakes out of the tin and garnish with chopped toasted almonds, if desired. Serve immediately.

Quick Cupcake Decorations

If rainbow sprinkles aren't your thing, there are other quick and cute ways to decorate icebox cupcakes. Here are some of my favorites:

✳ Make a pretty flower by placing a fresh raspberry on top of the cupcake and arranging sliced almond "petals" all around it.

✳ Hull some fresh strawberries and slice them into heart shapes for Valentine's Day.

✳ Cover the whipped cream with chocolate wafer cookie crumbs and plant half of a gummy worm in the "dirt."

✳ Tint the whipped cream pale green with food coloring, make some spiky "grass" by pulling upward from its surface with the tines of a fork, and place a Peep marshmallow bunny among the blades.

✳ Use seasonal candy instead of sprinkles for holidays: candy corn, pastel hearts, blue and red M&M's, or red and green M&M's.

✳ Use food coloring to color the whipped cream and plant a seasonal toothpick, available at party supply stores, in the center of the cupcake after frosting it with the whipped cream. Use green whipped cream and a shamrock toothpick for St. Patrick's Day, blue whipped cream and an American flag toothpick for the Fourth of July, etc.

blueberry and spice icebox cupcakes

Makes 4 cupcakes

I love the combination of ginger and blueberries, and this recipe is one of the simplest ways to get it. Whipped cream cheese gives the frosting of these pretty cupcakes some body but keeps it light. Be sure to refrigerate them for at least 3 hours, to allow the cookies to soften up. The recipe makes 4 cupcakes, perfect for a small dinner. You can easily double the recipe for a larger party.

1 cup fresh blueberries, picked over for stems

3 tablespoons sugar

1 cup heavy cream, chilled

¼ teaspoon pure vanilla extract

½ cup whipped cream cheese

12 gingersnaps

continued from page 136

1. Combine the blueberries and 1 tablespoon of the sugar in a nonreactive bowl and stir, mashing some but not all of the berries with the back of the spoon. Let stand for 15 minutes, stirring occasionally, to allow the sugar to dissolve.

2. In a large bowl, using an electric mixer, whip the cream, the remaining 2 tablespoons sugar, and the vanilla extract together until soft peaks form. Add the cream cheese and continue to beat until smooth.

3. Working on a baking sheet, spread about 1 tablespoon of the whipped cream mixture onto a gingersnap. Spoon a scant tablespoon of the blueberries on top of the whipped cream mixture. Top with another gingersnap, another layer of whipped cream, and another layer of berries. Top with a final gingersnap. Frost the top and sides of the cupcake with a thin layer of the whipped cream mixture. Repeat, making another 3 cupcakes. Cover the cupcakes with plastic wrap and refrigerate for 3 hours and up to 1 day.

4. You should have about 3 tablespoons of blueberries left over. Cover the blueberries with plastic wrap and refrigerate.

5. About 30 minutes before serving, remove the cupcakes from the refrigerator and place each one on a dessert plate. Just before serving, spoon a little of the remaining blueberries on top of each cupcake.

banana ice cream cupcakes with peanut frosting

Makes 12 cupcakes

Peanut butter and bananas make a great sandwich and an even better cupcake. When frozen, the fruit tends to lose some of its sweetness, so use a very ripe, sweet banana for the best banana flavor. To turn the cupcakes into a sundae-like dessert, remove them from the liners, place in dessert dishes, and spoon some Warm Chocolate Sauce (page 25) over them just before serving.

One 10- to 12-ounce store-bought pound cake, or 1 recipe Homemade Pound Cake (page 15)

1 medium-size banana, peeled and cut into ½-inch-thick circles

3 cups vanilla ice cream, softened

2 tablespoons (¼ stick) unsalted butter, softened

6 tablespoons smooth peanut butter

¼ cup confectioners' sugar

½ cup heavy cream, chilled

¼ cup chopped dry-roasted peanuts

continued from page 139

1. Arrange 12 paper liners in a 12-cup muffin tin. Cut the pound cake into ½-inch-thick slices. Use a 2-inch biscuit cutter to cut 12 circles. Place them in the bottom of the paper liners. Reserve the remaining pound cake and scraps for another use.

2. Combine the banana and ice cream in a medium-size bowl and mash with the back of a spoon to incorporate the bananas. Top each piece of pound cake with a scoop of the banana ice cream. Cover the muffin tin with plastic wrap and place in the freezer until the ice cream is firm, about 30 minutes.

3. While the ice cream is freezing, place the butter in the bowl of an electric stand mixer fitted with the paddle attachment and beat until light and fluffy. Add the peanut butter and confectioners' sugar and beat until smooth and well incorporated, 3 to 4 minutes.

4. In a large bowl, using an electric mixer, whip the heavy cream until it holds stiff peaks. Fold the whipped cream into the peanut butter mixture, taking care not to deflate the cream.

5. Remove the muffin tin from the freezer and cover the ice cream with the peanut butter cream (leaving the cakes in the tin). Cover with plastic wrap and return to the freezer to allow the topping to set, at least 2 hours and up to 1 day.

6. Remove the cupcakes from the tin and sprinkle with the chopped peanuts, pressing them gently into the topping. Let stand for 5 minutes at room temperature before serving.

mini coffee cakes

Makes 8 mini cakes

You can build perfect little quick desserts from mini Drake's Coffee Cakes. All you need is some coffee ice cream and raspberry jam. Use a sharp serrated knife to cut cleanly through the cakes. I like matching coffee ice cream and coffee cake (get it?), but you can vary the recipe by substituting different jam and ice cream flavors: Try apricot jam and vanilla ice cream, cherry preserves and chocolate ice cream, or orange marmalade and pistachio ice cream. Let the cupcakes stand for 5 minutes before serving, so that the ice cream starts to melt and soften up the cake.

1. Slice each coffee cake horizontally in half. Spread ½ teaspoon of jam over the bottom half of each coffee cake. Spoon 2 tablespoons of ice cream over the bottom of each cake. Place the top half of the cake on top of the ice cream. Wrap each cake individually in plastic wrap and freeze until firm, at least 1 hour and up to 1 day.

2. Unwrap and let the cakes stand for 5 minutes before serving on a platter scattered with raspberries.

8 Drake's Coffee Cakes

4 teaspoons raspberry jam

1 cup coffee ice cream, softened

Fresh raspberries, for garnish

mini doughnut ice cream sandwiches

Makes 8 sandwiches

These are absolutely adorable, a fun twist on the ice cream sandwich idea. With the marmalade and almonds, they make a great dessert for a casual grown-up dinner party. Substitute strawberry or grape jelly for the marmalade and multicolored sprinkles for the almonds, and they can be served at a kid's birthday or pool party.

1. Slice each doughnut horizontally in half. Spread 1 teaspoon of marmalade over the bottom half of each doughnut. Spoon 3 tablespoons of ice cream over the marmalade on each doughnut, making sure that some hangs over the edges of the doughnut. Place the top half of the doughnut on top of the ice cream.

2. Place the almonds in a small shallow bowl. Roll the sides of the doughnuts in the nuts, pressing the doughnuts into the nuts so they adhere to the ice cream. Wrap each cake individually in plastic wrap and freeze for at least 1 hour and up to 1 day.

3. Unwrap and serve straight from the freezer.

8 mini chocolate-frosted doughnuts

8 teaspoons orange marmalade

1½ cups vanilla ice cream, softened

4 tablespoons sliced almonds

brownie sundae cupcakes

Miniature snacking brownies form the base of these ice cream cupcakes for chocolate lovers. Any ice cream with some chocolate in it will work well here. The rich Chocolate-Caramel Sauce is nicely balanced by the salty cashews sprinkled on top.

Makes 12 cupcakes

12 mini brownies (such as Entenmann's Little Bites or Hostess Brownie Bites)

1½ cups chocolate, chocolate chip, or fudge swirl ice cream

1½ cups heavy cream, chilled

2 tablespoons sugar

1 tablespoon unsalted butter

½ cup salted cashews, coarsely chopped

Chocolate-Caramel Sauce

½ cup sugar

2 tablespoons water

¾ cup heavy cream

3½ ounces bittersweet or semisweet chocolate, chopped

1 teaspoon pure vanilla extract

continued from page 144

1. Arrange 12 paper liners in a 12-cup muffin tin. Place one brownie in the bottom of each paper liner. Top each brownie with a small scoop (about 2 tablespoons) of ice cream.

2. In a small bowl, using an electric mixer, whip the heavy cream and sugar until the cream just holds stiff peaks. Use a small offset spatula to cover the ice cream with the whipped cream (leaving the cakes in the tin). Cover the tin with plastic wrap and freeze until firm, at least 2 hours and up to 1 day.

3. Melt the butter in a small saucepan over medium heat. Add the cashews and cook, stirring frequently, until the nuts are browned and fragrant and have absorbed most of the butter. Drain on a paper towel–lined plate and let stand until completely cooled.

4. To make the sauce, combine the sugar and water in a small saucepan. Bring to a boil and cook the mixture until it turns a light amber color. Do not stir. If part of the syrup is turning darker than the rest, gently tilt the pan to even out the cooking.

5. As soon as the syrup is a uniform amber color, stir in the heavy cream with a long-handled wooden spoon. The mixture will bubble up. Remove the pan from the heat and stir in the chocolate until it melts and blends into the sauce. Pour the sauce through a fine-mesh strainer into a heatproof airtight container. Stir in the vanilla extract. Let stand until just warm to the touch but still pourable. (Chocolate-Caramel Sauce will keep, refrigerated in an airtight container, for up to 2 weeks. Reheat in the microwave for 1 to 2 minutes or on the stovetop until it is warm and pourable.)

6. Remove the muffin tin from the freezer and remove the cupcakes from the tin. Peel away the paper liners and place each cupcake on a small dessert plate. Spoon some of the sauce over each cupcake and sprinkle with the cashews. Serve immediately.

tortoni cupcakes

Makes 6 cupcakes

Here's a recipe given to me years ago by my good friend Beth Miller for an Italian-style semifreddo *dessert that's a lot simpler to make than ice cream. Serve these with Warm Chocolate Sauce (page 25) or Raspberry Sauce (page 35). Or top each cupcake with a dollop of sweetened whipped cream and some grated chocolate. Please note that this recipe contains an uncooked egg white, so, to be cautious, I don't recommend serving it to children, pregnant women, elderly people, or anyone in poor health or with a compromised immune system.*

1 large egg white

6 tablespoons sugar

1 cup heavy cream, chilled

1 tablespoon instant espresso powder

1 teaspoon pure vanilla extract

⅛ teaspoon pure almond extract

½ cup slivered almonds, toasted and cooled

2 tablespoons amaretto or other almond-flavored liqueur

1 recipe Warm Chocolate Sauce or Raspberry Sauce (optional; page 25 or 35)

continued from page 147

1. Line a 6-cup muffin tin with paper liners.

2. Place the egg white in a medium-size mixing bowl and beat with an electric mixer until foamy. Add 2 tablespoons of the sugar and beat on high, scraping down the sides of the bowl once or twice as necessary, until it holds stiff peaks.

3. Add the cream, the remaining 4 tablespoons sugar, the espresso powder, vanilla extract, and almond extract and beat until stiff. Fold in the almonds and amaretto.

4. Divide the semifreddo among the paper liners. Cover the tin with plastic wrap and freeze until firm, at least 2 hours and up to 1 day.

5. To serve, remove the paper liners and place each tortoni cupcake on a dessert plate. Spoon some Warm Chocolate Sauce or Raspberry Sauce over each cupcake, if desired, and serve immediately.

butterscotch petit fours

Chocolate cups made by brushing melted chocolate into foil mini-muffin liners are delicious containers for spoonfuls of rich butterscotch pudding with whipped cream on top. Steal one of your kids' unused paintbrushes to brush the chocolate evenly into the liners. Although these aren't technically cupcakes, they look like mini cupcakes because of the chocolate cups, and they're simply irresistible, so I had to include them.

Makes 12 petit fours

1½ tablespoons unsalted butter

¼ cup firmly packed dark brown sugar

Pinch of salt

1½ tablespoons cornstarch

1 cup half-and-half

4 ounces bittersweet chocolate, finely chopped

½ cup heavy cream, chilled

1 tablespoon confectioners' sugar

¼ teaspoon pure vanilla extract

Ground cinnamon, for dusting (optional)

continued from page 149

1. Combine the butter, brown sugar, and salt in a small saucepan. Cook over low heat, whisking, until the butter is melted and the sugar is dissolved.

2. Combine the cornstarch and ¼ cup of the half-and half in a small mixing bowl and whisk to dissolve. Set aside.

3. Add the remaining ¾ cup half-and-half to the saucepan and whisk until it is combined with the brown sugar mixture. Add the half-and-half-and-cornstarch mixture to the saucepan, stir to combine, and turn the heat to medium-high. Cook, whisking, until the mixture thickens, 3 to 4 minutes.

4. Scrape the butterscotch pudding into a heatproof bowl and cover the surface with plastic wrap, pressing the wrap directly onto the surface to prevent a skin from forming. Refrigerate until cold, at least 3 hours and up to 1 day.

5. Line a 12-cup mini-muffin tin with foil mini-muffin liners. Lightly spray the insides of the liners with nonstick cooking spray.

6. Put 2 inches of water in a small saucepan and bring to a bare simmer. Place the chocolate in a stainless-steel bowl big enough to rest on top of the saucepan and place the bowl over the simmering water, making sure the water doesn't touch the bottom of the bowl. Heat the chocolate, whisking occasionally, until it is completely melted.

7. Spoon 1 teaspoon of the melted chocolate into each muffin liner. Pick one up and tilt and rotate it to cover the bottom and sides with an even layer of chocolate (or use a small unused paintbrush). Place back in the muffin tin and repeat with the remaining cups. Spoon an additional ¼ teaspoon chocolate into each cup, tilting and rotating to cover any thin spots. Place the muffin tin in the freezer until the chocolate is set, about 10 minutes. (Chocolate cups will keep in an airtight container in the refrigerator for up to 1 day.)

8. Combine the heavy cream, confectioners' sugar, and vanilla extract in a medium-size mixing bowl. Using an electric mixer, whip on high speed until the mixture just holds stiff peaks. (The whipped cream will keep, covered with plastic wrap and refrigerated, for up to 6 hours.)

9. Carefully remove the chocolate cups from the muffin tin and peel away the liners. Place the chocolate cups on a serving platter. Spoon some pudding into each cup and top with a dollop of whipped cream. Lightly dust each cup with cinnamon, if desired, and serve immediately.

vanilla creme wafer mini napoleons

Crisp sugar wafer cookies with vanilla creme filling take the place of puff pastry in this quick version of a classic dessert. The little pastries are astoundingly pretty and fun to serve.

Makes 8 small Napoleons

½ cup stemmed, thinly sliced fresh strawberries

1 tablespoon strawberry jam

¼ cup heavy cream, chilled

1 tablespoon confectioners' sugar, plus more for dusting

⅛ teaspoon pure vanilla extract

1 tablespoon sour cream

24 vanilla creme sugar wafers

Mint leaves, for garnish

1. Combine the strawberries and jam in a small bowl and toss to coat.

2. Combine the heavy cream, confectioners' sugar, and vanilla extract in a medium-size mixing bowl. Using an electric mixer, whip on high speed until the mixture just holds soft peaks. Beat in the sour cream to combine.

3. Place 8 cookies on a serving platter. Spread each cookie with a heaping teaspoon of the whipped cream mixture. Cover with a layer of strawberries. Top with another 8 cookies. Spread each cookie with another tablespoon of whipped cream and top with another layer of strawberries. Top each Napoleon with a third cookie. Place the platter in the freezer for 10 minutes to firm up.

4. Just before serving, dust the Napoleons with powdered sugar and garnish with mint leaves.

strawberry coeurs à la crème with warm chocolate sauce

Serves 6

When I bought my beautiful heart-shaped coeur à la crème *molds (available at cookware shops), I swore I would figure out more than one way to use them. Here's my latest variation on the classic cheesecake dessert, using strawberries to tint the little cakes pink. I use crème fraîche, available in the dairy section of most supermarkets, for its delicacy and richness, but sour cream may be substituted if you like. Because no Valentine's Day dessert is complete without a chocolate component, I serve these with chocolate sauce.*

1 cup stemmed and chopped fresh strawberries

6 tablespoons confectioners' sugar

8 ounces cream cheese, softened and cut into 8 pieces

1 cup crème fraîche or sour cream

½ teaspoon pure vanilla extract

1 recipe Warm Chocolate Sauce (page 25)

continued from page 154

1. Cut a large piece of cheesecloth into six 6-inch squares. Wet them with cold water and wring out each square so it is damp but not dripping. Place a square inside each of 6 small coeur à la crème molds, with the edges overhanging the tops of the molds. Place the molds on a rimmed baking sheet.

2. Combine the strawberries and confectioners' sugar in the work bowl of a food processor and process until smooth. Add the cream cheese and pulse several times, scraping down the sides of the bowl as necessary, until smooth. Add the crème fraîche and vanilla extract and pulse once or twice to incorporate.

3. Divide the mixture evenly among the molds. Cover with the overhanging cheesecloth. Refrigerate the molds on the baking sheet until the excess moisture has drained off, at least 24 hours and up to 3 days.

4. To serve, remove the molds from the refrigerator. Peel away the cheesecloth that covers the top and invert each mold onto a dessert plate, gently lifting off the mold and the cheesecloth. Spoon some Warm Chocolate Sauce around each heart and serve immediately.

measurement equivalents

Please note that all conversions are approximate.

Liquid Conversions		Weight Conversions		Oven Temperatures		
U.S.	Metric	U.S./U.K.	Metric	°F	Gas Mark	°C
1 tsp	5 ml	½ oz	14 g	250	½	120
1 tbs	15 ml	1 oz	28 g	275	1	140
2 tbs	30 ml	1½ oz	43 g	300	2	150
3 tbs	45 ml	2 oz	57 g	325	3	165
¼ cup	60 ml	2½ oz	71 g	350	4	180
⅓ cup	75 ml	3 oz	85 g	375	5	190
⅓ cup + 1 tbs	90 ml	3½ oz	100 g	400	6	200
⅓ cup + 2 tbs	100 ml	4 oz	113 g	425	7	220
½ cup	120 ml	5 oz	142 g	450	8	230
⅔ cup	150 ml	6 oz	170 g	475	9	240
¾ cup	180 ml	7 oz	200 g	500	10	260
¾ cup + 2 tbs	200 ml	8 oz	227 g	550	Broil	290
1 cup	240 ml	9 oz	255 g			
1 cup + 2 tbs	275 ml	10 oz	284 g			
1¼ cups	300 ml	11 oz	312 g			
1⅓ cups	325 ml	12 oz	340 g			
1½ cups	350 ml	13 oz	368 g			
1⅔ cups	375 ml	14 oz	400 g			
1¾ cups	400 ml	15 oz	425 g			
1¾ cups + 2 tbs	450 ml	1 lb	454 g			
2 cups (1 pint)	475 ml					
2½ cups	600 ml					
3 cups	720 ml					
4 cups (1 quart)	945 ml					
	(1,000 ml is 1 liter)					

Index